Dennis Wood
On Another Beat
More True tales of a former Manchester Police Officer

P & D Riley

First published 2006

P & D Riley
12 Bridgeway East
Runcorn
Cheshire
WA7 6LD
England

ISBN: 1 874712 76 X

Copyright © 2006 by Dennis Wood

British Library Cataloguing in Publication Data
A catalogue record for this book is available from the
British Library

Printed in England.

About the Author

Dennis Wood served in the Manchester Police for a quarter of a century between 1950 and 1975, a period in which he saw a gradual change from what had been Victorian methods of keeping law and order by walking a local beat, to the situation we have today with police work being carried out by computers and officers in cars and all local contact with the public lost.

He entered the police service, as did many of his contemporaries, following military service with the Scots Guards during and immediately following World War Two.

Married to Sylvia, they have two sons, Nicholas and Richard. For many years Dennis wrote a column in Brief, the monthly journal of the Greater Manchester Police and is well known in the world of after dinner speaking.

His hilarious, true tales are typical of a period thought by many law abiding citizens as being halcyon, and there is no doubt that if Dennis and his former colleagues were in today's police force they wouldn't last a week because of all the regulations and red-tape that now takes the place in every British force of what was once called common sense!

This is the sequel to Dennis' best-selling first book *On The Beat*, which was first published in 2005 to great acclaim from police officers all over the world.

Acknowledgements

The author would once again like to thank Duncan Broady, curator of Greater Manchester Police Museum for supplying archive photographs for use in this book.

Many thanks also to members of The Caminada Society for raising long forgotten memories

Dedication

The author dedicates this book to all the members of N.A.R.P.O., The National Association Of Retired Police Officers.

Front Cover photograph:
The Author (left) with Alec Harris, a colleague at Greater Manchester Police Museum
Back Cover photograph: The author in the old charge office at Newton Street

Chapter One

The majority of the time spent walking around a beat was boring in the extreme, and the impression given by films or television to the contrary, a mere fantasy. Of course, in order to produce such programmes, a year of police activity must be packed in to half an hour. In reality, constables on their walking beats were obliged to occupy their eight hourly stints as best they could.

In the main, those duties which involved the daylight hours were alleviated by traffic control, or conducting children across the road to school. There were the occasional welcome breaks of course, like someone committing suicide or getting themselves run over on your beat, or the invitation to take a cup of tea at some place of business; then there was the hustle and bustle of the public all around as they went about their lawful business.

There was time to stop and chat and we spent hours listening to people pouring out their problems, often of some private and intimate nature, which they would never contemplate revealing to anyone else.

When most of the good people were in bed, and in the case of those residing in the close vicinity of what was then a highly concentrated area of heavy industry, coughing their lungs up all night, that's when the tedium would set in.

The night shift commenced at ten o'clock and terminated at six, and for a couple of hours there were incidents in which you may become involved, but in the main it would be a drag.

One of my colleagues, who in due course became a superintendent, frequently made his way to the main road junctions, where he removed his boots and knelt in them at the kerb's edge, his cape drawn about his shoulders. There were not many motorists around at night in the nineteen fifties, but those about to negotiate the junction, on spotting Norman, could be seen to swerve from side to side as they did so!

Those members of the indigenous population who had to get to the factories and mills by six in the morning, employed the excellent and reliable services of the 'Knocker Up'. These men, for a small fee, contracted to wake their clients by knocking on the bedroom window at the appointed hour. A long pole with a bunch of wires on the end was beaten against the glass, until the harassed and more often than not, angered, countenance of the customer appeared, at which, time, pole over his shoulder, he strolled on to his next annoying appointment.

Anyone who was a nuisance to the police and his neighbours would be treated to a long list of recommended punishments, not least the early call treatment. Such individuals tended to be work shy and therefore late sleepers. The officer on the beat would slip a note through the letter box of the 'knocker up' with a request ostensibly from the headache, to be awakened each morning of the ensuing week, at five. The innocent window pane rattler, when refused payment and threatened with violence at the end of the week, would recruit the aid of the man on the beat, and he would ensure that the headache stumped up the fee.

When, years later, along with everyone else, these nuisances found themselves in a position to own motor cars, and the duties of the knocker up became redundant, the avenging constables during the night, would quietly remove the hub caps from their vehicles, place a few pebbles in them and replace them. Great pleasure was derived by the morning beat man, who on the information from the night officer as to what had taken place, endeavoured to be in the street when the car was driven off to loud clattering as the stones spun round inside the hub caps.

Practical jokes against the sergeants were not to be recommended, as reprisals made life unbearable. At every major station there was a constable, usually getting on in service, who went under the title of the 'reserve man'. This officer was responsible for a number of duties, such as those of the station mortuary, the cells and their occupants, cleaning the offices and preparing the station officer's meals. It was an appointment much sought after by the older men as a form of convalescence from the ills of walking around in the elements over many years.

Big Archie, on his first week in that exalted role, was almost cast back in to the drudgery from which he had so recently escaped. Anxious to please, he concentrated on earning the approval of a station sergeant, who was, to say the least, difficult to please. He despised everyone and every thing, not least the haemorrhoids from which he experienced constant agony!

When on the morning shift, he would bring two eggs each day, which he left in the tiny kitchen area. It was the job of the reserve man to boil the eggs so as to be ready for consumption at nine o'clock precisely. He would go to a deal of trouble to instil that intelligence into any officer who had, for one reason or another, not carried out the task before, and to emphasise that they were to boil for a period of four minutes, not three or five, but four.

Big Archie, more than anxious to please, took the eggs on the first morning, and lowering them into the pan, covered them with water and with the concentration of a brain surgeon in action, supervised the culinary procedure until the water began to boil. He consulted his pocket watch and calculated that at eight fifty five he must take the eggs out of the pan and into the waiting sergeant. Some of the beat men were beginning to arrive in the kitchen, and Archie, at their behest, fed the fire with a couple of shovels full of coke. He chatted with the men as they consumed their refreshments, and a glance at the kitchen clock brought him up with a start.

Two minutes to nine glared back at him, and as rapidly as his huge bulk would permit, he transferred the eggs to a dish and to the table in the sergeant's dining area. He had barely reached the kitchen when a roaring from the dining room sent him back there.

The sergeant, eyes bulging, his great chest heaving, sat there. Before him lay the shattered remains of the eggs.

"Four minutes, I told you, four minutes!" panted the offended diner. "These must have boiled for a bloody week."

The persistent ringing of the telephone in the office, called the sergeant away and Archie saw no more of his tormentor that day. The following morning he kept away from the charge office and its grumpy supervisor as best he could, and discovering that the couple of eggs for that day's breakfast had been left as usual for him to prepare, he determined to do a first class job and to ignore all distraction until he had completed the operation to perfection.

Exactly as planned he boiled the water and lowered the eggs therein with a tablespoon. He remained at his post and to the consternation of those hoping to make use of the stove as they came in from the freezing outdoors, he precluded the facility of the instrument until a perfect pair of four minute eggs could be produced.

He removed the feast from the pan and into the dish. In the charge office, the sergeant rose to leave for his breakfast, and the clerk said, " I hope old Archie has got them eggs right today sarge."

"There wont be any problem today son," beamed the sergeant "I got the wife to boil 'em for me. I told the reserve man off nights to tell Archie not to touch 'em, I'm having them hard boiled!"

The pair of colleagues who assisted me in the gruesome business of removing the remains of a young man who had committed suicide, dreamed up a prank which taught me always to check everything before moving on to the next stage. It was a wet dreary evening, the rain which had been falling steadily for hours, still fell onto the streets and pavements, and on to the little railway station to which I had been directed.

"The driver of the 8.15 from Bury has reported hitting something on the line when he passed through Crumpsall Halt. Go and see if you can find out what it was," instructed the Duty Inspector.

I trudged along the line, trying, without success, to avoid a virtual minefield of puddles, the beam from my torch nipping from sleeper to line and ultimately on to a bundle which lay between the glistening rails a few yards before me. My first thought was that, as often is the case, some idiot had placed an obstruction there for a bit of fun. The bundle was not a prank. It was the body of a young man, decapitated, it seemed, by the rails of the train, the feet lying a few inches away, whilst the head was nowhere to be seen.

8

I moved the torso away from the lines and was joined by two constables, sent to assist. After some banter and grumbling from the pair, one of them went back to the station in order to inform the inspector and to arrange for an ambulance, which upon its arrival, I transported the body and myself to the mortuary at the divisional station.

Before leaving the scene, I asked my colleagues to search for the missing head and to bring it to the station in order that someone could identify the lad.

I laid out the remains on one of the mortuary trays and found several papers in the pockets of a jacket. There was an address and a note to the effect that the deceased had decided to end it all. I requested the police covering the appropriate district, to attend and ask someone to come to the station in order to identify the body. I repaired to the station canteen for a cup of tea, and shortly after, the pair who had been assisting me, turned up.

"We found the bloke's head," said one of the lads, pouring himself a cup from my jug.

"Must have been propelled like a football. Right up on the top of the embankment it was," said the other.

I asked where it was now and they informed me that they had placed it in the mortuary with the rest of the body. After thanking them as they returned to their respective beats, I was told that friends of the deceased had arrived. I greeted them and took them down the yard to the mortuary, on the way, putting them in the picture.

I entered the building, and some sixth sense told me to leave the party outside. The first shock was that the body was not on the tray where I had left it, the second was that it was in a sitting position, on a chair in the corner, the head under its arm and a cigarette dangling from its mouth. I had to place everything back in the correct order on the tray and cover it up to the neck with a sheet before I could invite the identification to proceed.

Few departments escaped from the practical joke brigade, as was discovered by an officer who had spent seventeen years in the uniform branch, and who on promotion to chief inspector, was transferred to the C.I.D. That in itself might well be considered a practical joke, as the C.I.D is a specialist department, wherein the daily work requires training and expertise, particularly in the case of its senior officers, who are regularly called upon to investigate major crimes, such as murder and to bring them to a satisfactory conclusion.

The chief inspector, overjoyed at his promotion, and the move, at once set out to furnish his wardrobe with the new uniform, that of a detective officer. The requirement, was a fawn raincoat, suit with waistcoat shirt, sombre tie and suitable shoes. An important accessory was headgear, the choice of which was governed by rank, so that all detectives up to and including sergeants were required to wear a trilby hat, and all ranks above, a bowler.

Striding in to the office on his first day, the chief inspector hung his raincoat and bowler on the pegs of a coat hanger immediately behind the main entrance and was shown to his office, a slight headache from the pressure of his brand new hat was quickly dispelled by a visit from the detective superintendent, which was by way of a half hearted welcome.

"He's bought it from Dunn's in Market Street," said the detective constable who had made a swift examination of the bowler. At the request of his colleagues he reported the size to be six and seven eighths.

A plan was devised which involved one of the detectives taking the hat to its place of purchase, with a view to replacing it on the hanger with a different size. The operation was carried out with smooth precision, and within the hour an exact replica of the bowler, two sizes smaller, occupied the hook on which the chief inspector had left it.

At six o'clock the same evening the office was unusually crowded, each of the officers apparently dealing with urgent paper work and none as much as casting a glance in the direction of the chief inspector as he proudly donned his bowler. Everyone pretended that they had failed to notice the unfortunate victim as he struggled in an attempt to force the undersized hat to remain in place. In the end he left the room nonchalantly holding the offending article in his hand.

The next morning, a little after nine, he hung the headgear again on the hook and repaired to his office. An inspection revealed that the hat had been replaced, the original size ticket giving evidence there had been an early visit to Dunn's. A conference appointed a different officer to exchange the bowler and a decision was made that another branch of the hat store be used for the transaction.

"There's one at Rochdale," offered the C.I.D. clerk, and the switch was completed within the hour.

"What size did you get,?" enquired one of the sergeants.

"Eight and three quarters," announced the courier.

"It'll come down on his shoulders," said the sergeant.

The prediction was almost spot on when the owner placed the garment on to his head. It fell completely over his eyes and was instantly removed, to a chorus of the foulest profanities on behalf of its wearer, followed by a commitment to a nearby pedal bin. The chief inspector was spared any further humiliation, when it was discovered that his move to the detective branch had been an error at the time of his raising in rank, when the chief constable, having polished off three quarters of a bottle of scotch, got him mixed up with a detective inspector, who had spent the first two weeks as a chief inspector hurtling up and down the motorways in the transport department.

The colloquial name for the grim and sinister Mill Street Police Station, was 'Madison Square Garden.' I have no idea why, but over its century of existence those who dwelt within its jurisdiction had so named it. The only other building of that title is in New York and is where tough guys meet their match on a regular basis, often being in receipt of second prize, and wishing they had kept out of the place to begin with.

The ugly crowded streets and dwellings which stretched for miles around the station accommodated the work force which was important to the high concentration of industry there, and the volume of pollution in the air they breathed, settled daily on everything and everyone, young and old alike. Detective Chief Inspector Eric Jones, on hearing he was to be transferred from the comparative suburbia of Didsbury, to the Mill Street office of the C.I.D., was horrified and protested that he had no old clothes to wear. He need not have been so concerned as the existing members of the department, ignored the environmental condition, and went to work in sartorial elegance, a dead giveaway when propping up the bar in one or other of the myriad pubs.

When I went to work in that office, I found there was no lack of light relief, with the obligatory leg pulling of a newcomer in plentiful supply. Searching for a file, I discovered, in a cupboard, a white coat with a stethoscope dangling from its pocket.

" It's for when anyone in custody asks to see a doctor," explained one of the detectives. "One of us puts the coat on and the stethoscope round his neck and..." I walked away, not wishing to show that I had fallen for the gag, and avoided asking about the barrister's wig and gown I later discovered in a drawer.

Many of the wheezes were cruel and went beyond harmless jokes, as with that perpetrated against Detective Constable Terry Fagan. The duty of 'night detective', carried out in turn, involved a week as the sole detective on a division, between the hours of eleven at night until seven in the morning. It was only occasionally that there was anything to do and most made use of the period to catch up on their mountains of paperwork.

Terry settled down in a remote area of the station on the first night, and ploughed in to his backlog. In the morning, he decided to visit all the C.I.D. offices before going home. As he entered the superintendent's office he was taken aback to find it full of pigeons. The birds had all but covered the room with their droppings, and to add to the situation dozens of candles, having been lit earlier, had now burned out and had scorched the areas in which they had been standing. The boss's desk had been the most affected. Terry, having a limited amount of time in which to tidy the room, set about the task with zeal, to no avail.

The detective superintendent, not known for an even temper, arrived in time to see the last of the pigeons being removed from the scene. No time was lost in blaming the matter on Terry, though after the boss calmed down to a mere fit of rage, he conceded that Terry, being the only detective in the area all night, would hardly have been foolish enough to do something knowing that he must be the only suspect available. In the end the room was better than new and Terry was off the hook. There were plenty of suspects of course, but in those days there were no fears of a colleague informing on you and the truth never got out.

The Fire Brigade and the police, having been a single body for many years, became independent of each other a few years before I joined the force but both services continued to be on excellent terms with each other, throughout my time. Should you have the good fortune to have a Fire Station on your beat, you were welcome to join the lads for a game of snooker and a cup of tea as they relaxed between call outs. It was weird to be taking a shot on the green baize when the alarm bell sounded, to find your opponent, and everyone else, scatter to the engines. and leave just you and the duty fireman, the only people in the station.

All around the streets of Manchester were devices named game wells, green metal stands with a small handle on the front. The idea was, that should anyone require the fire services to attend an emergency, they merely turned the handle and a signal would be received at the nearest fire station. The process noted the location of the signal and the engines turned up there, hopefully to find the person having activated the alarm, in a position to indicate the venue of the fire. Wilfully activating the game well was an offence, and a plaque on the pillar plainly pointed that out. In the main, improper use was quite rare, though there were occasions when soup heads would take pleasure in ringing them in for a joke. They invariably remained nearby in order to enjoy the frustration of the firemen when they discovered they had been duped.

Whilst having a quick smoke in a deep doorway one sultry evening, I saw a well known trouble maker approach a game well, take a careful look around, then turn the handle. He then crossed the road walking towards my temporary haven, presumably to watch the show in comfort. As he entered the doorway, I grabbed him, and a brief struggle ensued, followed by my dragging him over to the scene of his stupid prank.

The bells of the fast approaching engines grew louder and the idiot pleaded with me to overlook his behaviour, to no avail of course. Two engines came to a halt, the crews of both being well known to me. I introduced the man who had called them out, just for fun, and they took him off my hands and in to one of the vehicles which was driven off, followed by the other.

When I again called in to the fire station some fortnight later, I mentioned the incident and asked about the soup head.

"Don't know anything about it," they chorused.

Sent to a fire some months later, I found that the brigade had been called out to a house in a fairly well to do district. On my arrival I saw a leading fireman with whom I was friendly.

"It looks bad," said my friend. "Electric plug in a bedroom started it and fortunately we got here in time to extinguish it before it managed to engulf the whole of the property."

He directed me up the staircase and in to a smoke filled bedroom, where I saw that there was a figure in the bed, the smoke stained bed linen drawn over the occupant with the long hair of a female cascading on to the pillow.

"Dead?" I enquired, to which the leading fireman nodded.

"Husband must have gone off to work earlier and left her asleep. I've sent for him and he should be back here very soon."

The crew packed up at the scene, leaving me to what would be required by the Coroner. I returned to the bedroom in order to inspect the body, in case of obvious foul play. The smoke had practically all gone and I leaned over the bed to withdraw the sheets. The sight before me was for a couple of seconds, puzzling.

The 'spouse' of the absent tenant was one of those mannequins more normally to be seen in the windows of fashion shops. It was in the days before 'blow up dolls', and I could only assume that the gentleman, now ascending the stairs, had in some way or another, found the model to be the perfect substitute. He seemed a harmless soul and I avoided any mention of his partner. The report was brief, and I forgot about the circumstances, until I saw my mate, the leading fireman again.

"His wife wasn't dead you know," he laughed.

"No that's right," I said, "just one of those quiet ones."

Chapter Two

The grim Victorian edifice within the grounds of Crumpsall Hospital, began life as one of the major workhouses in the city. There were many such institutions and in the absence of the handouts available today, they did serve a purpose. Anyone who fell upon hard times may well find themselves an inmate of the workhouse, where, in return for a twelve hour day of back breaking work, they would be provided with shelter and a very bland diet.

Those unfortunates, once taken in, rarely got out again, as to successfully do so would require an income with which to acquire shelter and sustenance, not to mention clothing, as they would be made to surrender the garments issued by the institution.

The Grubber, as the workhouse was colloquially referred to, had cast off its old image of purgatory by the time I became familiar with it, and was operating as Springfield

A police tug-o-war at Bruche Training Camp, Warrington, in 1950

Mental Hospital. Some hundred or so beds were occupied in the rambling wards. It lay, in the centre of twenty eight beat, and a six week tour would bring that beat officer to its door on numerous occasions. The main purposes of the visits were to conduct enquiries on behalf of His Majesty's Coroner, which involved every patient who died whilst at the institution.

The reports seldom used up more than a dozen pages in our notebooks and there were seldom any relatives to give evidence of identification, one or other of the staff obliging. Often, it transpired that the deceased had been at the hospital for many years and had never been suffering from a mental illness as such, but had more likely been only a little retarded, or an epileptic, conditions, for which happily, today, there are medications and excellent care available.

On nights, when there was a full moon, it was eerie to walk through the grounds as the inmates would be wailing and howling. A long standing member of staff informed me that the phenomenon had originally given rise to the term 'lunacy' as in lunar.

In nineteen fifty six, when serving a spell in plain clothes, I was given an enquiry to pursue on behalf of the police at Glasgow. They were endeavouring to trace a man whom they believed was a patient at Springfield in order to eliminate him in a missing persons enquiry, and for that purpose I presented myself to the office. A check with the office manager revealed that the individual was a patient, and had been so for some ten years. I asked to see him and was informed that he was in ward thirty two.

"You'll never find him on your own, it's such a rambling place," said the woman, turning to a smartly dressed young man in crisp white coat who at that moment had entered the office.

"Malcolm will show you," she said.

I followed my guide along the dimly lit ground floor, through several rubberised doors which slammed together as we passed through them. Up a flight of stairs and along again through more doors. Through wards in which patients incoherent tirades were directed towards me, together with threatening poses by inmates adopting fighting attitudes. Malcolm quickened his pace until we were almost running through those distressing wards, until, he having burst through double doors just ahead of me, disappeared from view. There was a distinct absence of any other nurses or orderlies and I was obliged to traverse the hospital wards again, at long last gaining the front office, where sat the manager.

Malcolm was standing by the fireplace, hands deep in the pockets of his overall.

"Find him all right?" she asked.

"No I didn't," I replied. I went on to explain that my erstwhile guide, having led me all over the hospital, left me stranded on the fourth floor.

"Oh Malcolm you are naughty, apologise to the policeman at once," she said.

"Is he one of the patients?" I asked. There was a nod of assent from the manager and a wide grin from Malcolm. I went back to the C.I.D. office and informed Glasgow accordingly.

During my service there was an unwritten rule to the effect that policemen were welcomed by bus and tram crews, to ride, in uniform upon those vehicles without having to purchase a ticket. It benefited both factions, the coppers for obvious reasons, the drivers and conductors, particularly at night when they were obliged to convey belligerent drunks from place to place. The hitherto peaceful route from the city centre to Middleton, became a nightmare when the new council estate was built on the rural setting of Langley, just north of that small township.

Most of the original people of Miles Platting, their homes being under clearance orders, were re-housed at Langley and settled down to a foreign environment very well. One problem was that those removed from the area of the railway shunting depot, were unable to sleep in the silence of the countryside.

A great many remained loyal to their regular water holes in the Manchester area and each weekend returned there in order to fill up with the brands of ale to which they had become accustomed over many years. That was where the bus crews came in. If a police officer didn't own a bicycle on which to travel to and from work, he was on public transport, and when, after the three to eleven shift, he boarded a bus to go home, particularly at weekend, he invariably became involved.

"Right you bastards," the conductor yelled, directing his remarks to the upper deck as I boarded his bus at Harpurhey one evening. "There's a copper got on, now let's hear what you've got to say, you so called tough guys."

I stood on the platform of the vehicle as the little guard ran up the stairs and I could hear him remonstrating with the drunken passengers.

The driver left his cab and joined me. "It's that Langley crowd again," he said, lighting a cigarette. "Every Friday and Saturday it is."

The noise upstairs grew louder and there were shouts of "police." I climbed the steps to find the conductor was underneath a pile of struggling bodies. Sometime later, having rescued the tiny official, I directed the driver to take us all to Willert Street Police Station, where, with the assistance of the office staff, I took half a dozen of the main culprits off the bus and in to the building, where they were charged with being drunk and disorderly. The remaining, well behaved and respectable passengers continued on their journey.

Having missed the last bus, I had to walk the three miles to my home, thereby getting in to bed around three o'clock in the morning. Though we were supposed to travel to duty in full uniform, I avoided doing so thereafter, by wearing my civilian raincoat over the uniform and carrying my helmet in a shopping bag. Of course this action resulted in having to pay my fare, but it was well worth it. Two or three years after deciding to travel incognito, a colleague was on duty in Newton Heath when a passing cyclist informed him that a man had been set upon by a gang of thugs at New Cross, some mile and a half away. It was in the days before personal radios and the like, so the officer leapt upon the platform of a passing bus, the route of which would pass the scene. He had no idea that the car immediately behind the bus was being driven by a superintendent from another division.

When he alighted the superintendent enquired as to whether he had paid his fare.

"No sir," he replied, and went on to give the reason.

"What fight?" he asked.

New Cross was deserted and he was forced to admit that he had failed to secure the particulars of his informant. At a hearing before the chief constable, he was fined a hefty sum, to be taken from his wages, to be paid in weekly instalments over a long period of time. The effect of that punishment was to cause everyone to insist upon the operatives taking their fares.

In due course wage rises enabled the purchase of old bangers and motor scooters. Evolution permitted the officers to house their uniform clothing in lockers at the station. Conductors were withdrawn which resulted in the drivers tending to ignore what was happening to those who were temporarily in their charge, and who could blame them?

In the case of the Langley bus route, the nostalgic visits to old stamping grounds lost its appeal, and the good people of Langley became citizens of Middleton. The last occasion that I waited at a bus stop in uniform was one Saturday evening, having retired from duty on the three to eleven shift, and as I took my place in the queue a large black saloon car drew up and I was surprised to see my father in the front passenger seat.

"Come on get in, we'll give you a lift," said my dad. I placed myself in the rear seat and found myself sitting with a smartly dressed man, who was extremely drunk and who persisted on leaning against me throughout the journey. My father's friend, who was driving, informed me that the drunk was his business partner.

"He's not used to drinking," said my father, who was. "Called in a few pubs in town with him and he's gone over his limit by the look of it. We'll drop him off at his house, then we'll drop you off, unless you want to call at the White Hart for a night cap."

I turned down the invitation, in the knowledge that it would be the early hours of the morning by the time I got home, plus the fact that being in uniform, my presence in a hostelry of after time consumption, would no doubt prove uncomfortable.

The vehicle drew up outside a large detached house in a tree lined avenue, and at the request of my father, I dragged the half unconscious man from the car. The journey along the drive to his front door seemed never ending and I was glad to let him slip from my grip to the door step where I pressed the door bell then returned to the waiting conveyance. The following day, my father telephoned and furnished me with his drunken companion's number.

"Can you call that chap's wife?" he asked. " She insists that he was brought home in a police car and he insists that he wasn't. She says the shame is unbearable and refuses to leave the house in case the neighbours witnessed the performance." I said that I would, but afterwards decided to let sleeping dogs lie.

The purchase of a push bike for the princely sum of ten shillings a month, over ten months precluded any repetition of accepting lifts from anyone again, at least when in the full regalia of a guardian of law and order.

"Answer the phone will you?" said the elderly station officer. We were in one of the small section houses which were to be found scattered about the division, open twenty four hours of the day, each being manned by a constable, usually getting on in years. As the officer was in the tiny kitchen, clearing up the crockery which had been used by a couple of the lads earlier, I obliged. It was a routine message which I entered in to the desk journal before joining the old chap in a cup of tea.

"Thanks lad," he said. "Whenever I leave the office the blasted phone rings." I suggested leaving it off the hook and he said he was prepared to endure it, as being a station officer was far better than walking about the streets in the rain.

"I've only got four years to do and there's no bloody telephone going to lose me this cushy little job, not like it did for old Frank Daley. It was a good bit before you joined and old Frank, who had waited years for a duty which would keep him indoors, finally made it as the station officer here in this very building."

"What happened?" I asked.

"Well, he was on nights and half way through his first week in here. Everyone was out , and about two in the morning he nodded off at the desk, just as the phone rang. He picked it up and being half asleep he could hardly make out what the bloke on the other end was saying. It was the police at Blackpool, who after several aborted attempts, managed to convey that a Mrs. Lever of number eleven Thomas Street, having been on a day trip to the resort, had missed the coach and was stranded. The request was for Frank to go round and tell her husband."

I was due back on my beat, but anxious hear the rest. However, the storyteller was in no hurry and I was forced to hang on whilst he filled his pipe from a pouch of some ancient origin. He leaned back in his chair and half closing his eyes, smoked with the enjoyment of a man to whom a pipe is a rare luxury.

"What he did," continued the station officer, "was to put his helmet and overcoat on, lock up this place, and go round to number eleven Thomas Street. When Mr. Lever answered his knocking, he told him his wife had been 'strangled' at Blackpool! There was a hell of a fuss the next day, after Mr. Lever, who had spent a fortune on a taxi in order to collect his very much alive spouse from Blackpool Central Police Station, when, as he later pointed out in a letter to the chief constable, she could have got home on a single train ticket costing a couple of bob."

I got up to leave and asked what had happened to Frank.

"Back on the beat of course, and stayed there for the rest of his service," replied the station officer. As I stepped in to the street I could hear the telephone ringing in the office and called back to the station officer that I hoped it wasn't another call from Blackpool!

Police constable Alan Adamson was one of a number of officers to have achieved twenty five years devoted service, without the trouble of having to attend court in order to present evidence against anyone.

"I did actually try charging someone once, but I got a bollocking, which sort of put me off ever trying it again," he told me.

"Everybody makes a few mistakes early on," I said.

"Sure they do, but this was when I'd been in the job for five years," he replied. He went on to relate the incident, which had taken place when, having called in to Ancoats Hospital in order to use the toilet there, he was informed by the Casualty Sister that she was currently treating a young man who had been brought in with lacerations to his wrists.

21

"He's been telling me that he is fed up and wants do away with himself," said the sister.

Alan had not absorbed a great deal with what had been crammed in to his head at the training school those five years before, but, for some reason, a period on suicide had managed to stick. He knew, for instance, that any successful suicide victim would be free from prosecution, but that to attempt to commit the act was a criminal offence. The poor lad, having been in receipt of the expert skill of the sister, was immediately arrested.

Sometime later he was propped up behind the desk at the station, where it was the duty of the sergeant to examine the evidence before accepting any charge.

"I charge this man with attempting to commit suicide sergeant," began the constable.

"That offence was repealed, taken off the statute books, two years ago," murmured the sergeant.

The prisoner was released and Alan went back on to his beat.

"I've never bothered since," he told me. He did, however, continue to be one of those characters, to whom something untoward is always happening. Shortly following his retirement, he was invited to stay with relatives in Oldham and on Saturday evening, his hosts went out for a drink, leaving him with a bottle of rum and a video to watch. About ten o'clock he was startled to hear deafening pop music coming from the house next door. There was no let up from the thudding screeching racket which seemed to be at its loudest when his relatives returned from the pub.

"It's that bloke who's just moved in, he was doing it last Saturday as well," yelled his brother in law.

Egged on by his wife, and seven pints of lager, he left the house in order to remonstrate with the musical tormentor. Within a few minutes he returned, sporting a torn jacket, together with a pronounced limp and several facial bruises, the 'music' having increased in volume to warn any other protesters.

Alan, also fortified by drink , and a sense of duty towards his relatives, went outside. He saw the neighbour standing on his drive and immediately drove a clenched fist into his ribs. The neighbour, making a remarkable recovery, caught

Alan a beauty full on the nose. A battle ensued in which the injuries sustained by the brother in law, were soon surpassed by both combatants and the fighting carried on until his host, at the insistence of his wife, came out to see what was happening.

"What are you doing?" yelled the battered relative, limping up the drive and forcing himself between the combatants. "This is Mr. Pearson from next door but one."

Alan's adversary clung to the gate post and explained that he had been approaching the front door of the inconsiderate neighbour in order to complain about the music, when he was set upon by the maniac who was clinging to the other gate post fighting for his breath.

All three retreated to the brother in law's house to bathe their wounds and finish off the rum. When they at last bade each other goodnight, it was to the accompaniment of the thumping 'music' crashing through the walls from next door.

Among the sprawling streets and tightly packed terraced houses of Miles Platting was a moneylender's office, which was in effect, a terraced house, though the proprietors lived in a much less grimy district, and outside the hours of business, the premises were listed on that beat, as requiring special attention. A huge safe occupied the centre of a rear ground floor room, and the man on the beat had to look through a window in order to see that all was in order. So that the officer could get in to the rear yard, a catch had been rigged up in a special way, which involved reaching over the gate in order to release it.

On one of those very cold mornings when icy conditions prevail, I left the station at six o'clock and reached the beat about ten minutes later. A sudden and pressing need to visit the toilet had me quickening my step, not to where I should have been at that hour, but to the yard of the moneylender, which had that facility. Most people, when carrying out their employment, have no such problem, but on the beat there are few, or no, conveniences, and to return to the station for such purposes, involved entering in to a book the reasons, together with the exact time taken during the visit, the details always considered to be an unnecessary time wasting exercise.

I entered the yard and quickly did what had to be done,
I then discovered that the frosty conditions had caused the
outside toilet flushing mechanism to freeze up. There being
nothing that I could do, and being a fair way from where
I ought to be, I secured the yard gate and slid along the
icebound pavements towards that rendezvous.

It was to be two hours later that I returned to the area
of the moneylender's place, by which time, he and his wife
were in attendance. As the lady always made a pot of tea
for the officer on the beat, I entered the office.

"I'm glad you are here constable. I was going to ring the
station," said the proprietor.

"We've had visitors during the night," said his wife.

I suddenly realised that in my haste I had not actually
examined the premises, being preoccupied at the time, and
asked where they had got in.

"No, they weren't burglars. Come on I'll show you," he said,
leading the way to the outside toilet. He pointed out to me
a situation I was already aware of.

"Get me a bucket of hot water," I requested and off he
went, to return shortly afterwards with the steaming vessel.

"What are you going to do?" he asked as he backed away.
I poured the boiling water into the lavatory, after which it
was crystal clear.

"I know you fellers get some rotten jobs to do," the grateful moneylender said, "but we both think you are wonderful." He pressed a pound note in to my hand, a small fortune in those days, which of course I handed back to him.

"If we can't help anyone in difficulty we may as well not
be here," I said, as I stepped out onto the street with a
distinct feeling of a job well done.

Chapter Three

I collected a railway warrant, which was to be my ticket, for a journey to the Devonshire town of Newton Abbot, one Monday evening in the bitterly cold month of January nineteen fifty one. The purpose of the trek was to enable me to give evidence at the local magistrates' court, in the case of a man charged with a minor motoring offence, whom I had interviewed on behalf of the Devonshire Constabulary, at an address in Manchester some couple of months earlier.

As I took the required statement from the motorist at his home, it transpired that he had been on a family holiday which had involved driving through Newton Abbot, and whilst he was unable to recall having done so, had failed to give way at an appropriate traffic sign.

"I shall be pleading not guilty to this" said the interviewee.

His small daughter, who had been gazing at me throughout my presence, stood up, and presumably not to be denied an opportunity of reporting something to a policeman who was something of a captive audience, said out loud "My daddy wee-weed in the sink!"

The effect was electrifying, and immediately after her daddy had penned his signature, I left. The journey began at a snail's pace as the train nosed its way out of London Road Railway Station to Stockport, the first stop of what seemed to be hundreds on the long haul southwards. The carriages were without heating and my feet became the first part of my body to notice it. Gradually the intense chill travelled throughout the whole of my anatomy, a torture apparently shared by my travelling companions.

As I had been made aware when frequently being herded around on troop trains, it was a wise move to be armed with a bag of sandwiches and a flask of tea on such occasions. After crawling along for some three hours, I partook of the refreshments I had brought with me, to the obvious envy

25

of my fellow passengers, who, it seemed, had not thought of similarly arming themselves.

Having been up since five o'clock that morning, I lapsed into a fitful slumber and was spared the freezing experience of the next few hours until reaching Tewksbury, which one of my companions confidently assured us, was in Gloucestershire.

There followed a long delay, the reason for which, as is the case even today, was kept secret from us. The remainder of the journey continued in the same vein, until around five thirty in the afternoon, when we came to a stop at Newton Abbot. I disembarked and waved to those who were to continue the nightmare until reaching Exeter, then trudging through the now swirling snow I found the local police station.

After introductions I was escorted to a small bed and breakfast establishment in the main street, and there, in turn, to a Spartan bedroom by the landlady "Don't allow no drink nor smoking in my house," wheezed the landlady, as she drew deeply on a cigarette. "If you was to go out you must be sure to be back before I lock up at ten."

The room was even colder than the railway carriage I had recently escaped from, and when I inspected the old fashioned washing bowl and jug on the dressing table, I discovered that the water had frozen. A chamber pot lying underneath the bed hinted to me that there would be no access to a bathroom. I had been furnished with the price of accommodation at the time of receiving the rail warrant.

"And I want a receipt when you get back," the inspector had said.

It crossed my mind that the very few shillings of my own might be well invested in a sleeping draught, but a glance through the window at the deserted street and its virgin snow, put me off from searching for a pub and instead I partly undressed and placed myself under the refrigerated bed sheets.

I was up and dressed, though not very successfully, washed and shaved, long before the obnoxious old girl called me down for breakfast. I think the repast had been cooked in second hand lamp oil, but I was so hungry I devoured the half warmed mess before me.

"There's your bill," croaked the creator of the meal. I paid her the vastly inflated sum of seven shillings and five pence and retained the document, so much in demand by the inspector. I found my way to the courthouse by nine o'clock and after a long wait in the draughty corridor I was approached by the Court Inspector.

"You P.C. Wood from Manchester?" he asked. I told him I was and he informed me that the defendant I had come to give evidence about, had pleaded guilty by letter and I was no longer required.

The journey back to civilisation was no less uncomfortable than that of the day before, and that night I was in my own bed. The following morning I turned up for duty and after presenting the inspector with his receipt and handing him the change from the ten shillings he had given me, I stepped off on to my beat.

"All right for you," said one of the lads on the section. "Having it off in glorious Devon while we're covering your beat for you." I asked him to go away, in words to that effect.

Very few of the men I worked with could be accused of panicking or losing it under any of the horrendous situations which regularly confronted them. Counselling, with a few weeks off sick in order to recover, had not yet been invented, though there were many, including myself, who would be prepared to take advantage had it been, as there was always a requirement to carry out painting and decorating at home. Mangled corpses and the like looked just as gruesome in the nineteen fifties as they do today, yet none of us was prepared to let anyone else know if we happened to experience a slight queasiness.

My wife would always be aware that I had been dealing with a fatal accident which involved a child, as I was apparently subdued for a day or two, but that was the only outward appearance most of my colleagues would reveal. There were however circumstances wherein the facilities afforded to the crew of the Star Ship Enterprise, that of being spirited away on a cosmic beam in order to avoid embarrassment would have been greatly appreciated.

When Sir John MacKay became the Chief Constable, he arranged to see everyone who had qualified for promotion, howsoever long before he came to office. Being amongst those who had been overlooked for years, I was ordered to avail myself. I enquired from a constable who had been interviewed some couple of days earlier, as to the form of things.

"You are marched in and stand in front of the chief," said the officer. "There's all the Watch Committee with him on a long table, and they all ask questions about you." he went on.

I asked whether there were any surprises, and he informed me that the chief had been asking everyone for their suggestions for the improvement of his force. Armed with the advice, I attended for interview some days later, and in answer to the bombshell, I made the point that as both the fire service and the police had to submit reports relating to fatal fires, it was unnecessary duplication, and that as the fire officers were more able to assess what had occurred, the police should not have to waste time reporting also. The chief mumbled something about it being a mute point, and that brought the ordeal to a close.

When I returned to my division I met P.C. John Cooper who was to be interviewed that afternoon. I acquainted him with the format, giving him plenty of time to prepare, and the following day I asked him how he had got on.

"When he asked about improvements, I said that the crime bulletins displayed on the station notice boards daily would be much better if, in addition to such information as appears in relation to the crimes, the name of the detective to whom the crime had been allocated could be shown, and in that way, the constable on that beat would be able to pass any information directly to him." he said.

I remarked that the suggestion was a good one and enquired as to the chief's acknowledgement of it.

"He said it had its merits, though he wondered whether all the beat men looked at the bulletins on a daily basis, if at all. He asked me if I looked at them regularly and I told him that I certainly did."

John went on to say that the chief fixed him with a prolonged stare. "You may like to hear that what you have suggested this afternoon, has in fact been carried out during the past two months at my instigation!"

I have so often wished to be spirited away from all forms

of embarrassment, not least on an occasion when the very same chief, accompanied by one of Her Majesty's Inspectors Of Constabulary, was being driven along Knowsley Street in Cheetham in order to visit the section station there. I was walking out of the building as they drew up at the kerb and seeking to impress the pair, I executed a perfect salute. In my enthusiasm, my fingers struck the brim of my helmet with such force as to send it flying from my head and in to the road, where it rolled for a fair distance, then came to a stop on a grid.

The chief didn't say anything, but merely stared at me, as he had at P.C Cooper. A short time after those promotion interviews, I was transferred to a department where the uniform was discarded for twelve months and all duties carried out in plain clothes.

One sergeant and six constables was the complement, the individuals returning to uniform and being replaced at scattered intervals over the year. I partnered an officer for two months then his replacement, Joe Robson, became my side kick for the ensuing ten months. We got on well together, playing and working hard throughout the period of the partnership.

At first, I was a little apprehensive, especially when he accompanied me in to one of my favourite pubs on the first evening.

"Two pints of bitter ?" called the publican, as we entered the bar.

"No, I'll have a tomato juice," said Joe.

"Stop messing about," said mine host, as he held the pair of pint pots at the ready.

" I don't drink," said my colleague, almost apologetically. It hadn't occurred to me that I could have been given someone to work with who was a teetotaller. It has to be said that by the end of our association, he was as good a boozer as anyone I have ever met.

Plain clothes sergeants, usually had a pet subject which they were inclined to concentrate upon during their year in office, and for ours it was brothels. Others were obsessed with the licensing laws, illegal betting and gaming and so on, but ours, for some reason, brothels.

Now the successful prosecution of persons who are the

managers of such venues is one of the most difficult things to achieve and involves long weary periods of observation whilst crouching behind walls etc., usually at the mercy of the elements. This procedure had to be kept up for at least a week, before there was enough in your notebook with which to persuade a magistrate to issue a warrant for a search of the premises and to arrest the brothel keeper.

"I want you to take observations at this address," whispered the sergeant, showing us a piece of paper on which the address of a run down hotel was written. We both knew the place well, as it was frequented by most of the villains in Manchester and was owned by one of the most notorious amongst them.

There was a bar in the basement in which alcoholic drinks were supplied at grossly inflated prices until the early hours of the morning. However, the main attraction was the several prostitutes who packed the bar and entertained the customers in the grubby bedrooms on the three upper floors.

It would be the most difficult operation to carry out a full scale raid on the premises, and some twenty or more police officers, including policewomen, would be a minimum requirement. Joe and I had, a few weeks earlier, attempted unsuccessfully to get in to the hotel by pretending to be Italian sailors from a ship at Salford Docks The two lumps of wood on the door told us, in a most uncouth manner, which had we really been Italians would surely have upset us, that we couldn't come in.

On the first night of the observations, around ten o'clock, we crept through the churchyard which lay directly opposite to our target and in between the old grave stones nearest to the road, settled down for a long watch. It was a little early for the punters, though we noticed one or two whores whom we knew, as they arrived for work. Somewhere around ten to eleven we heard the sound of someone walking on the pebbled drive to our rear and lay perfectly still as the crunching of the stones drew nearer. Through the darkness I could make out a shadowy form, which spoke.

"Where are you lads?" it asked. We got to our feet and approached the figure. It was the owner of the hotel with two steaming mugs of coffee.

"Here you are lads," he said. "You must be bloody freezing out here."

He left coffee on a grave then disappeared as mysteriously has he had arrived. Some time later, based on the numerous attendances of prostitutes, a warrant was issued and duly executed. Firstly, the apes on the door were literally picked up and temporarily carried away. Then the raiders swept in to conclude a very well conducted operation. The subsequent court hearing resulted in stiff fines all round and the forfeiting of the drinks licence. The identity of whoever it was that had forewarned the hotel proprietor was never discovered, though the name of a particular officer came up frequently and years later, when I saw the individual out socially, I thanked him for the coffee. He didn't take the trouble to reply.

I had never worked from the old police station in the city centre, which is now the Greater Manchester Police Museum, but I know that during its ninety nine years as a busy station it was the scene of many unusual happenings. In the old days, policemen carried a leather dog strap in an inside pocket of their tunics. The instructions pertaining to stray dogs were to the effect that all such unfortunate creatures, when pointed out by a member of the public, were to be captured and taken to a police station, entered in to the stray dogs journal, and housed in one of the cages kept in every station yard.

A vehicle was in attendance each morning to convey the guests to the Dog's Home. Often, when things had gone quiet, around three o'clock in the early hours, the sergeant would try to enjoy a nap, only to be kept awake by those stray dogs caged in the yard as they howled in protest at their incarceration.

The station sergeant would go into the yard and ask them to be quiet and a refusal to comply would result in them mysteriously escaping, only to be brought back in by zealous constables who had found them wandering in the streets. Sometime around the end of the nineteenth century, constable Tony O'Donnell was patrolling his beat at midnight, when he came across an unusually large dog at the rear of the Gaiety Theatre. The beast was stretched out over the pavement dozing and paid little attention to him as he slipped the noose of his dog lead over its head. He dragged the animal to its feet, and with a few sharp words, accompanied by a gentle kick, persuaded it to walk at his side through the deserted streets. He strolled in to the charge office where his companion immediately rose and placed a huge pair of paws on the counter. The clerk and the sergeant, transfixed for a split second, sprang to life and raced for the back door. Both officers, being of ample proportions were momentarily jammed in the portal and arrived outside gasping for breath. With great presence of mind, the clerk slammed the door closed and then joined his senior who was looking in to the office through a window.

"What is it sergeant?" panted the trembling clerk.

"It's a bloody lion, that's what he's brought in," answered the sergeant. "Go and tell him to lock it in a cell," he ordered.

The clerk was seriously considering disobedience, but the consequences of a return to working a beat drove him to a degree of valour he had no idea he was capable of. Gingerly, he returned to the office and from behind a cupboard, passed on the explicit instructions he had been given, without revealing the conclusion to which the sergeant and he had arrived with regard to what was on the end of the lead. The animal quietly accompanied P.C. O'Donnell into cell number one, where it was at last safely detained..

The charge office sergeant made a dignified return to his post to enquire from the officer, the circumstances surrounding the occurrence. It was not until they had all gone home and the morning shift were in office, that the matter was resolved. The noble beast was appearing at the Gaiety in an animal act. The stage door had been left ajar and it had merely strolled out.

"She's a lioness actually," explained her owner. "All the animals in the show are tranquillised and she would be far too sleepy to attack any of you."

The old girl was again tranquillised by her owner and returned to the theatre in a Hanson Cab in time for the matinee performance. Constable O'Donnell was back on duty that same night, with a vow to stay off the beer for a while!

Where you find groups of men working together, you find

nicknames, and the police force is no exception. In the Manchester City Force were:

Off at one John ...An inspector, who when on the 5 pm- 1 am. shift, was bound to respond to a need for his presence at any time after 9 pm, with "I'm off at one, get someone else to attend."

Lord Effingham ... A verbose senior officer, whose use of the "F" word was religiously sustained.

Vinegar Jim ... A very pleasant soul, undeserving of his acidulous features.

The Editor ... A constable, famed for his enthusiastic use of the truncheon.

Bootsey ... A constable of impressive stature, blessed with size thirteen boots.

Omo ... (a popular soap powder of the day) A timid inspector, with a fetish for cleanliness, both physical and spiritual.

Chorlton Ghost ... A probationer constable. Who on three occasions on a winter's night, remained unseen by his sergeant, despite being on view to the general public.

Idle Jack ... Of which there were many. They knew who they were, and they knew we knew.

Bucket Head ... Those officers whose helmet was far too big for them.

Thirsty Fred ... A sergeant who was extremely fond of beer.

Toby Jug ... A constable with an uncanny resemblance to one.

The Black Widow Spider ... A policewoman with a special type of demeanour.

Big Daddy ... A sergeant of massive proportions, of whom we shall hear more later.

The Baron ... A constable named Charles Rothschild.

Biggles ... A constable who was a former fighter pilot.

Sparkler ... A constable who arrested two small children who had purchased fireworks whilst being under age.

If you were unfortunate to qualify for a nickname, it was to remain with you until death, and for many years after.

The young man who had recently taken out a mortgage on a small terraced house in the Newton Heath area , was almost too overcome to speak to myself and the sergeant who had joined me in the investigation of a burglary at the address. The house was totally unfurnished, though a great effort on the part of its new owner had been made to thoroughly clean and decorate every room. The front ground floor room was particularly fine, the wallpaper being of a light cream with a satin design of vertical stripes.

The sergeant enquired as to whether anything had been stolen.

"All I had in here was an old clock which was on that mantle piece, and that's gone," said the lad.

I went in to the kitchen to take a look round and I could hear the sergeant asking further questions.

"What's the description of this clock?" he asked. "Did it have Arabic numerals or Roman?"

The young man answered that the numbers on the clock were neither, but were in fact, English.

I heard the sergeant say "were they like this, or like this?"

The lad answered that they were similar to the first one.

I came in to the room and saw that drawings had been made on the freshly hung wallpaper, of various clock faces and numbers.

"Did it have a round or square, or even rectangular face?" asked the sergeant, as he drew examples all over the walls.

The tenant took the ball point pen from the artist and in one of the few remaining spaces, he drew his own version of a description of the absent timepiece. We took our leave, with a promise from his tormentor, to the effect that every effort to trace the clock would be made.

By mere chance, the sergeant saw the stolen clock in the window of a second hand shop, the proprietor of which was a well known receiver of stolen goods, and though he protested that he had no idea from whom he had purchased, raised no objection to the officer taking possession of it. The next day it was returned to its grateful owner, who made no mention of the mural.

Chapter Four

The Special Constabulary, was, as their title suggests, indeed something special. They are a group of individuals who in their own spare time, and without payment, get dressed in the uniform of the regular police, except that a flat cap was worn instead of a helmet, and the matter of height was less of a restriction. These brave lads could turn up for duty at any time and the section sergeants were obliged to allocate a patrol area for them.

They were of course, less highly trained than the real police, but in many cases, a great deal more enthusiastic, which unfortunately caused a lot of extra work for the man on the beat. Some of the specials would become involved with situations which, though minor to begin with, could turn in to all kinds of a complication within minutes, resulting in the officer on the beat becoming entangled in a matter that might well have been resolved by diplomacy and tact.

I turned up at the divisional headquarters for the night shift on a Christmas eve and decided to pack my whole section of six constables in to the patrol van, which had a radio. Individual officers on their beats on festive nights were fairly ineffective as, having no means of contact, there was no way of gathering enough men to deal with large scale fighting, and on the eve of 'peace and goodwill' such battles were many.

On the section was an entertainment centre which encompassed, six large dance halls, each with a bar, and two large pubs. The complex guaranteed some ten or more thousand merry makers at any weekend, a figure perhaps doubled over the festive season, and it was the intention to park up on the forecourt to await the inevitable.

As I was piling the constables in to the radio van, the night inspector called me over. He had with him one of the special constables.

"Here sarge," he said. "Mr. Kilner has come to help us out and I'd like you to take him in the van with you."

The rest of the party gazed with incredulity on the special and when I announced that he would be with them all night, there were mutterings, not entirely under the breath, as to where they would be if they could choose on a Christmas eve.

En-route to my destination the driver drew up outside a shop at which the intruder alarm was in operation, and through the grill which separated his cab from the area in which we were travelling, he informed me that it was a shop which sold large sets of scales.

"The glass is broken in the front door, but nobody could get in," he said. "Anyway, they'd need a giant crane to lift anything in the place."

I got out and formed the same opinion. Nevertheless, the procedure those days was to stand by the premises until the key reference was alerted and attended. I knew very well that on a Christmas eve, we would never get anyone to come out, and if that was the case, I would have to post one of my valuable men there until the reference could be found, probably the next day.

Calls were beginning to come in about disturbances and I made the decision to post Mr. Kilner at the front of the shop, with an instruction not to go away until further notice. A flurry of snow was developing as we sped to the entertainment centre and as the van came to a halt on the esplanade, we piled out and in to a group of fighting youths. The vehicle, soon loaded, left for the station, whilst the remainder of us set about persuading others to go home, pointing out to defiant ones that we were insisting, with the toe of a boot. As the night wore on, there were those other Christmas specialities in the shape of serious assaults, fatal road accidents due to drunken driving, and the obligatory fatal house fire, again often the result of over doing the consumption of alcohol.

I soon became involved in such occurrences and about six o'clock in the morning, I called for the van to pick me up and take me back to the main station. On the way through the now quietened streets, the driver asked me whether the special constable was still at the scale shop. I had to admit that I had forgotten all about him and directed the officer to proceed there with all haste.

To my relief he was still at his post, the alarm still clanging away. The poor man was frozen, having stood there for almost eight dreary hours.

"I have been trying all night to find someone to come down and see you," I lied. "We'll take you back to the station now and I'll send someone else here."

At the station I thanked him profusely and after wishing him a very merry Christmas, signed the rest of the team off and went home, to sleep through the festivities there.

Every Chief Superintendent was entitled to be driven to and from work in the divisional car. It was a task which usually fell on the divisional clerk, as he was invariably one of the few officers to hold a driver's licence. Our chief superintendent, not being the owner of any form of transport, availed himself of the facility on a regular basis, and woe betide any officer whose duty it was to pick him up at eight o'clock each morning, who turned up any later.

He was a difficult man to understand, and it was doubtful that he appeared on the Christmas card list of anyone junior in rank to him. Those who were in line for promotion feared him worse, and when P.C. Rower, who was temporarily filling in as clerk, received instructions to go and pick him up, he was almost too nervous to drive anywhere. His passenger lived some twenty miles away and the traffic, due to an icy fog, was hardly moving.

The procedure, he had been informed, was to wait outside the house, and when the boss got in to the rear seat, to drive and not speak unless spoken to. He drew up outside the address at 7.50 and waited as ordered. The front door of the premises was opened and a stout lady, wearing a pinafore beckoned the officer to come in. The constable hesitated, having regard to the strict instructions he had been given. The woman repeated the signal, and believing that the chief superintendent had asked her to send for him, he tentatively complied.

Once inside the woman told him to sit down at the table.

"You must be almost frozen out there lad," she said, setting down a mug of steaming tea and two slices of toast.

The officer could hear the clumping of footsteps from the room above, which he interpreted as being those of his chief. He saw from the clock on the kitchen wall, that it was two minutes to eight and heard that the footsteps had been transferred to the staircase.

"Don't worry about him," said the boss's wife. "He'll have to wait until you've finished."

All efforts to devour the scalding beverage, and the toast were failing, made worse by the now presence of the divisional commander. He was fully dressed in bowler hat and raincoat,and staring at him unblinkingly without a word.

Throughout the journey, which felt more like two hundred miles rather than twenty, there wasn't a single word uttered, though he was informed later that his silent passenger had made up for it as he entered the station, finding fault with everyone within hearing distance throughout the rest of the day.

Over the next couple of weeks P.C. Rower waited for some form of retribution, which never came.

"Perhaps his dear wife marked his card," I offered.

I was with the same officer on nights sometime later when we discovered that the front door of a grocery store had been forced open and almost off the hinges. We had a good look round inside and finding the premises was not hiding the burglar, I asked my colleague to go back to the station and cause the manager to be informed. I remained inside the store to await his return.

Within a few minutes, I made out the figure of a man in the doorway. I remained still and saw him look up and down the road and then step inside the shop. In the darkness he stumbled around and when he reached the cigarette display he began to fill his pockets. He turned to go back to the door and I grabbed him, just as the divisional van attended with Constable Rower aboard.

"Hello Jack," said the van driver, on seeing the prisoner. "You only came out last week didn't you?"

I asked the van crew to take him to the station and tell the inspector that I would be over to charge him later, then P.C. Rower and I went back in to the shop to await anyone else who might be after the commodities therein.

"The manager's been told and he's on his way down," said

the officer. We waited for about ten minutes, when we saw a figure walk past the window, to return seconds later, and without hesitation step into the shop and stride confidently across the unlit floor in the direction of our hiding place. I caught the intruder by his left wrist, whilst the other constable grabbed his right. There followed a series of ear piercing screams as he attempted to wriggle himself free, after which he became limp and slid to the floor. I said that as soon as the manager turned up we'll get him to board the door otherwise the cells are going to be full tonight. It was my turn to go and make arrangements with regard to the van, and when I entered the station the clerk asked me if the manager had turned up, to which I replied in the negative.

"Funny," he said, "he was here a little while ago, left his car in the yard to walk over to you."

I hurried back to the shop, to find the other officer rendering first aid to the 'thief'.

"He's the manager," whispered my colleague."

"Yes I've figured that out," I replied.

We dusted him down and when he was fully recovered, he said he hoped we gave the same treatment to every burglar.

"Something like that, yes," said P.C. Rower.

The breathalyser was introduced around nineteen sixty seven, and before that people who were suspected of driving whilst under the influence of intoxicating liquor, were subjected to a rigmarole reminiscent of a pantomime farce. The chances of the offence being proved in court were very slim, as all sorts of similar symptoms and effects could very well be present in a multitude of medical conditions, a point often leapt upon by lawyers who specialised in the subject.

Up until the breathalyser, I had dealings with only two alleged drunken drivers. Happily, the first one only caused damage to himself, a lamp post and his own Ford Cortina. The procedure was to take your prisoner to the divisional headquarters where a police doctor was sent for. The doctor required the alleged drunk to walk a straight line across the office, notes being recorded as to his ability to do so without falling over. He would be asked to repeat one of those tongue twisters, which most teetotallers would find an exact-

ing task. Other tests of eye reaction would bring the examination to a close, and the doctor would then give his opinion as to whether the subject was under the influence or
not.

In my first case, the driver pleaded guilty, but on the second occasion of my involvement it failed to reach even the
preliminaries. At one o'clock in the morning, I was standing
with the inspector at the junction of two major roads just
outside the city, when he pointed out to me one of those
oversized American cars travelling towards us on the wrong
side of the road at what was almost a walking speed. The
nearside wheels were bumping on and off the kerb every few
feet. We stepped in to the carriageway and to our relief, the
vehicle came to a stop. I opened the car door and immediately recognised the driver as being one of those popular
wrestlers who entertained the nation every Saturday afternoon on television.

The inspector asked him to get out and as he complied,
he took the keys from the ignition. Neither the inspector or
myself could be described as small men, but the obviously very
drunken man before us towered above our own height his
huge frame swaying from side to side as he leant against
the roof of the car. He wore the clothing of a native
Canadian, and his hair was in the style of that noble tribe,
the Mohicans.

The inspector told him he was being arrested for drunk-
en driving, at which he took great exception, and brushing
us both aside, he squeezed himself back behind the wheel.
When he discovered the inspector had possession of the
keys he became most annoyed and after a great deal of
argument, he agreed to go to the station, provided the
inspector let him drive him there, which he did.

As we pulled in to the yard, I jumped out and ran to
the canteen where I recruited half a dozen officers who were
taking their break, explaining the situation on the way out.
The inspector was outside the car and promptly ordered all
assembled to help him take the passenger to the charge office.

There followed a deal of pushing and pulling, not to mention puffing and blowing, terminating in the successful extri-
cation of the muscular power house. He stood at the side
of the vehicle, where he executed a war dance, during which

40

we all took hold of a limb apiece.

"Watch out he's full of firewater," yelled the inspector. There followed a mighty struggle, which though it lasted a mere couple of minutes, took it's toll in the shape of minor cuts and bruises all round and culminated with the awesome giant lying face down in a cell.

Of course, the inspector, having allowed him to drive, could no longer proceed with the normal course of events, and about noon that day, when it was considered he was fit to drive, the chap was released. Nothing more was ever heard from the wrestler, and the matter was kept fairly quiet, although those in the know were in agreement that the right thing was done, if only to stop the man from killing himself, or more importantly, somebody else!

Whilst those of us in the front line, so to speak, got on with our often difficult and dangerous tasks, there was the small beginnings of a bureaucratic monster in Whitehall which was destined to grow and grow until the police force became unrecognisable. After all, the vast majority of the citizens ask only to be assured that the police are on hand when they are experiencing what is to them a traumatic event, and not to be told, by someone who may not even be a police officer, that it is not a priority.

As to standing on the street on a wet night and being expected to fill in a set of forms in order to justify speaking to someone carrying a sack on his shoulder, the mind boggles, and for the forms to be endorsed with the detainee's comments on what he thought about being stopped. What would the person say? "Thank you I really enjoyed that."

My experience of those early tremblings was to be sent for when I was a sergeant and to be informed that an anonymous letter had been received to the effect that Adolf Hitler, far from dying in a bunker in Berlin in nineteen forty five, had in fact escaped and was living in Openshaw, a district on the division.

He was to be found on most evenings, the letter said, in the Half Way House, a popular pub in the area. I laughed out loud, only to find the superintendent with a serious expression.

"There is a recent instruction which you seem to have missed, which states that all letters, anonymous or otherwise

41

are to be looked in to and a report submitted on the outcome," he said.

I did pop in to the Half Way House, but it wasn't to look for the fuhrer. All in all, it wasn't until I was nearing retirement that the Bleeding Hearts and Libertarian Brigade began to emerge, making life easier for the habitual criminal.

There were still plenty of colleagues who, intentionally, or otherwise, provided amusement. Police constable Andy Willow, who it must be said, enjoyed a glass of beer.

"Purely medicinal," he would say. "I get a bit depressed on nights when there's nowt doing, and a couple of pints cheers me up."

Of course his nocturnal dodging the column was well known to the sergeants and inspectors: anyone above those ranks was tucked up in bed and consequently had little interest as to what went on in the dark.

On a particularly foggy night, both the inspector and sergeant decided to make an effort to trap the wily Andy, red handed, and by eleven thirty they hid themselves in the close proximity of one of the ale houses he was known to frequent.   Around midnight they were rewarded when a glimpse through the swirling fog, found the door opening and the appearance of the landlord on the step. At his side was the huge Irish wolfhound, which, well known to everyone on the division, he was in the habit of taking round the block before retiring. The animal, likely to have caught the scent of the pair, gave a gentle though purposeful growl and the publican, sneaking a glance, caught sight of the reflection from the inspector's cap badge as he pressed back in to the doorway opposite, at which man and beast went back in to the premises.

Andy was told of the observation, and dismissing any suggestion of escaping by the back door, in the likelihood of the sergeant waiting there, another equally fraught scheme was discussed, and in the absence of invisibility being an option, it was decided to go ahead with it.

The collar and lead was removed from its proud wearer and transferred to Andy's neck, then the officer, holding his helmet close to his stomach, wrapped his cape around his body.   The landlord opened the front door and detecting the reflection of the inspector's cap badge again, led the hapless constable, who was now on all fours, along the footpath, turning left into a dark passageway which led to the main road. The officer stood up and removing the dog collar, replaced his helmet and sped off in to the direction of Stevenson Square, the location he should rightly be patrolling.

The inspector, seeking to avoid embarrassment, ordered the sergeant never to mention the episode to anyone, and the sergeant, having met the licensee on his return to the back entrance of the pub failing to ask where the wolfhound was, agreed.

It was not difficult to incur the wrath of the supervising officers and even the most conscientious in the ranks were deeply criticized from time to time.

Constable Ken Hamlet, as reliable an officer as you may find in any police force, was selected by his section sergeant for a job requiring tact and diplomacy at a church function one Saturday evening.

"They're having a dance and they don't want any gate crashers, so you stand at the door and see to it that they don't. Me and my family attend the church and the Parish Priest is a personal friend of mine," ordered the sergeant, who was renowned for his unreasonable attitude and violent temper.

Ken turned up at the church hall precisely at seven thirty to find several of the parishioners putting the finishing touches to the decorations and arranging the chairs around the walls. He was greeted by the parish priest and introduced to several middle aged ladies with blue hair, one of whom brought him the obligatory cup of tea which she placed on a table at the hall's entrance.

Gradually the partygoers began to arrive, each handing over their ticket to him and passing through to the hall., from where the scratchy tones of a Victor Sylvester record could be heard. By eight o'clock the ticket holders were all inside, with the exception of a group of giggling teenaged girls who had gathered in the foyer and were talking to the priest.

The group remained in the foyer for some twenty minutes, then at the suggestion of Father James, disappeared in to the main hall leaving the constable to his lonely vigil. There

43

had been no one trying to gain entrance without tickets, and at ten fifteen, Father James came to see him with one of the girls who had been earlier congregating in the foyer.

"Would you put Teresa here out of her misery?"

Teresa a pretty seventeen year old, trying in vain to disguise her admiration of him, stood, hands behind her back in anticipation.

"She would love to have a dance with you," he explained.

Ken, was about to explain that he was unable to leave his post, when Father James volunteered to take over for a few minutes The imploring expression on the face of his admirer found him escorting her to the dance floor, where a waltz was in progress. To a round of applause from the other waltzers, he swept the girl on to the floor, and although his being in full uniform , complete with thick soled boots was inhibiting, he began to enjoy the experience.

After having executed a particularly difficult manoeuvre he found himself looking at the sergeant, who was standing at the entrance to the hall. A quick decision had him completing the dance and walking his partner back to her group. The sergeant, who was waiting in the foyer, was red faced and appeared about to go off like bomb.

Fortunately, Father James joined him before the explosion.

"Now William," he said to the sergeant. "I insisted that he danced with your daughter as a favour to me," he said.

The intervention calmed the sergeant down remarkably swiftly and within seconds he told the constable that he could go home from there and that he would take over until the function finished. The incident was never spoken of again.

The old divisional headquarters of the B Division, built around eighteen eighty, nestled amongst the highly populated streets of Collyhurst, to the Northwest of the city. Through the division ran the districts of Cheetham, Crumpsall, Blackley, Moston, Newton Heath, Miles Platting, Collyhurst and Ancoats. The indigenous population were employed in the abundant factories and mills, though most of the males in the Newton Heath area earned their living on the railways, on a round the clock rotation system.

It was for the first thirteen years of my service, the perfect training ground, and I took full advantage.

The number of constables, sergeants and inspectors on the

44

division was around two hundred and seventy and there were thirty eight beats, all but three which were worked on a bicycle or on foot.

It seemed there were policemen everywhere, both night and day, and all this commanded by a Superintendent and a Chief Inspector. At the termination of my police years , the division was run by a Chief Superintendent , two superintendents and four chief inspectors.

The superintendent, when I came to the division, and the chief inspector, were busy each Thursday making up the wages of those under them, apart from that they found plenty of time to be out and about. The superintendent had a favourite hostelry in Moston, where he could be contacted if need be, and his deputy was always conspicuous as he rode his cycle all over the division.

The bike was fitted with a delivery basket over the front wheel which was nearly always full to capacity. His unwritten rule was never to salute him when he was riding, as due to the weight of the contents of the carrier, he was unable to return the compliment. To do so would no doubt cause him to lose control of the machine and down would go chief inspector and piles of commodities collected on his travels.

Though it may seem today to have been an inefficient way of policing such a large area, law and order was well kept by men who knew how to do it. To be fair, when comparing modern day policing, our hands were not tied by the bureaucracy and the charitable fads of the do-gooders which seem to have been designed to make certain that the criminal appears to be the afflicted, whilst the victim is in the wrong.

Chapter Five

The police force has, since 1919, been banned from forming a trade union, and if any officer was so much as to discuss the prospect of forming one, or taking any sort of industrial action, he or she would find themselves in very serious trouble, and may even finish up in prison.

Having said that, there is a federation, which in itself, is a toothless tiger. Every police officer is invited to join, and nowadays there is a separate federation for officers who are not white.

The organisation has its representatives amongst the rank and file who are devoted to the welfare of their serving colleagues. In the old days these representatives had to work shifts, just like the rest of us, and were somewhat resented by the senior ranks, as being trouble makers. Often, they engaged in appearing on behalf of officers who had become the subject of a disciplinary hearing before the chief constable and because of their vast knowledge of the regulations, they were often successful in getting the charges dismissed.

Police constable John Cowan, was the federation man for the force, a man of keen resolution, having accepted the role, determined to stir up as much opposition to the senior ranks as he could. When Sir John MacKay became the chief in nineteen fifty nine, P.C. Cowan was pressing for the traditional capes to be replaced by light weight raincoats. He set out to make a thorough nuisance of himself in the matter, and at every opportunity, he would be down at the chief's office to respectfully argue the case. On one of these occasions, Sir John said that he appreciated the difficulty which the officer had in dealing with all these circumstances, whilst working nights etc.

"I have therefore decided that you shall have an office here in headquarters, and that you will, as from today, work normal office hours."

John was no fool, and from that moment, until the day he retired, he became less and less of a nuisance to the higher ranks.

Much earlier on, John and I were standing at the corner of one of those high class avenues, built by the Victorians, to house people who were in professional occupations and in business in the city. Little that was anything to do with the police ever occurred in the area and we were surprised to hear a series of blood curdling screams from a house about half way along the tree lined thoroughfare.

We hurried towards the direction of the ever increasing screams and eventually through the open door of the location. In the spacious lounge an elderly man lay sprawled in an easy chair, and staring at the ceiling. Leaning across a grand piano was a woman, and it was from her surprisingly petite frame that the powerful howling was emitting. There not appearing to be any immediately identifiable reason for such distress, I dashed upstairs and through every room. There being no one up there I came back to the lounge, where to some extent the screaming had diminished, and John was being put in the picture.

I went outside and informed the gathering neighbours that everything was under control and on my return, the man of the house had begun to outline the reason for his wife's condition.

"Take your time Mr. Brovski," John advised.

The old man, between gasps, told us he had for many years, been the proprietor of a modest jewellery shop in the city and had retired some years ago. He had no children to carry on the business so the shop was sold.

"A few weeks ago," he continued, "we met a nice young man and it turned out that he was a displaced person and came from the very same town in Russia which we had left many years before."

Mrs. Brovski, having by now partially recovered, added that they had invited the pleasant young man to their house, where he had been staying ever since.

"After about five weeks he mentioned that his father had been a collector of rare coins, and after his death he had inherited them," said her husband. The old jeweller asked the lad what had become of the coins and to his surprise, he was told that they were here in Manchester.

"I put them in the property office at London Road Railway Station and they gave me a ticket so I might collect them anytime," he said.

The old man, struggling to contain his excitement, enquired as to how he had managed to get them past the authorities, all the way across the continent to England.

"I acted to everyone that I was of simple mind and before I left I rolled each coin in to a ball of plaster which I rubbed in mud so as to dirty them all. Every time I was asked about the stones I said they were from the grave of my beloved father", was his explanation.

The retired jeweller, trying to compose himself, volunteered to value the contents of the stones and enquired as to what sort of coins they were. The refugee said that they were all one hundred rouble marked seventeen twenty and of course

On the beat in Rochdale Road, Manchester

48

solid gold.

The expert waited a couple of days then reminded his lodger that he had not yet brought the coins for him to value. A further frustrating week, during which he had consulted a friend, who was an authority on the subject, as to the value of such currency, found his head reeling as the opinion was some £800 per coin. That evening he came right to the point and informed the lad that he had already priced the coins at £20 each.

"How many are there?" he asked, straining to be casual about it all.

"There are twelve," answered the lodger.

There followed a definite arrangement for a transaction to take place the next evening and the vendor produced a brown paper envelope, in which, he requested the cash be deposited. The next twenty four hours passed with agonising slowness till at last the lad arrived and placed a small, but heavy sack down on the polished dining table. He took out a couple of stones and at once, broke them open to reveal two of the promised coins.

The old man took the coins out of the room where he tested them, and finding them to be a good quality gold, returned to the lounge. He passed over the brown paper bag in which he had deposited £240 in brand new one pound notes, and the young man placed it in to an inside pocket of his well worn jacket. The seller then began to crack up another of the stones and was firmly requested by the lady of the house, not to do so because of the mess.

The jeweller, having lost none of his distrust for business transactions, politely required the lad to leave the cash with him until all the coins had been examined. The lad, equally politely took the brown paper envelope from his pocket and left it on the piano. He announced that he was going out for a while and left the house. A further inspection of the stones revealed an absence of any further coins which he found annoying, though not altogether distressing because the money was lying on the piano.

Mrs. Brovski, opened the package to reveal two hundred and forty pieces of newspaper, each the size of a one pound note.

"That's where you came in," her husband told the officers.

No trace was ever found of the con man, though from time to time, over the years, his description and method of working cropped up on the various national crime bulletins as he relied on the greed of his victims to earn a nice living.

The prevention of crime has been one of the main purposes of every police force since Sir Robert Peel introduced his Metropolitan Police in eighteen twenty nine. At one stage of my service I became a Crime Prevention Specialist and as such, had access to all kinds of sophisticated instruments with which to deter skulduggery. There were special chemical products, which when applied to an object such as the interior of a purse, left unattended, showed up on the fingers of a person who had fished around in it without the authority of its owner. I had occasion to visit a police station which was many miles away from my own, where the crime prevention officer was well known to me. He had asked for my help, in the shape of my newly acquired closed circuit television camera.

The machine was devised to allow a record being made of anything which took place within the area it covered, over an eight hour period of surveillance.

"I've got a problem with trying to discover what's going on in the canteen at this station," he told me over a cup of tea. A glance round the room revealed a battered old billiard table, five chairs, each of some ancient origin, an electric water heater for brewing up and a couple of dozen cracked cups and plates.

"The superintendent had me in yesterday and told me something in strict confidence, and now I'm telling you, because I want you to lend me that camera you've got, just for a couple of nights."

I told him at first that it would be impossible, as my own boss might call on it's use at a moment's notice, and then, seeing that he would only have it for a couple of nights, I relented.

"Someone," he began, with a quick look around for eavesdroppers, "someone, who is in the group which is on nights this week, has found a way to by pass the meter that regulates the lights over the billiard table, and the buggers are using it without paying. It usually takes about £6 a week, but when this lot are on it's lucky to take a quid."

I decided that if the camera was fixed in an upper corner of the room behind an already present bowl of dusty artificial roses, it would escape the notice of anyone interfering with the wall meter.

"Who has access to the keys of the meter?" I asked.

"Only the inspector," he replied.

"Well make sure it's working when he goes up," I advised.

In due course the camera was installed and I went over everything with my friend.

"The tape runs for eight hours, so you can view the next day. If there is no result, rewind and set it up for the next night and so on, and I must have it back by weekend," I insisted.

The following day I received a call from the officer to the effect that the machine had done its job and that I could have it back.

I drove the twenty odd miles to pick up the instrument and once safely stowed in the boot, sat down to listen to the result of the experiment.

"Worked like magic," announced my pal. "My boss would like to keep the tape if you can manage it."

As I had a ready supply, I agreed, and then he unfolded the facts.

"Put it all on at eleven, and took it off this morning at seven. Then, in the superintendent's office, he and I watched the tape." he said.

He went on to describe in full the faithful record of the night's events. Saying that there was nothing to see but the empty room until the clock on the wall showed midnight, then, in walked the inspector, who, without hesitation, took a key from his pocket and opened the light meter box. The table was illuminated and he set up the billiard balls, at which stage a policewoman entered and joined the inspector in a game of billiards. I said that he was lucky to obtain the proof he was after and got up to leave.

"No, you haven't heard it all yet," he said, and continued the account with beaming smiles. "The game was suddenly abandoned and the inspector was seen to turn the key in the canteen door, then return to the table, upon

51

which the policewoman was reclining. There was a great deal of cavorting and wrestling, and after some five minutes, an adjustment of uniforms by both parties. The inspector, having reactivated the billiard light meter, left the room and the object of his short lived affections, made herself a cup of tea and partook of her sandwiches.

"When the boss saw all that, he switched off the recording and sent for the policewoman, who by then, was at home and sleeping. On her arrival in his office, he told her what he knew of her behaviour of the night before, though not about the tape. She told him that she was very sorry, but that she and the inspector had been something of an item for many months."

The image I had of the scene had set me off laughing and I made my apologies for interrupting the account, given with much seriousness by my friend.

"There's more mate", he said and went on to say that the superintendent asked the girl to wait outside and asked him to play the tape a little further on, to which he complied. The further revelation was that the policewoman was seen to finish her refreshments and to be joined by a sergeant, who at once took her in to his arms and bestowed a series of kisses on her lips and neck.

"Then there was a repeat performance of the earlier exhibition at the billiard table," said the crime prevention officer.

"The superintendent ordered me to play the tape to its end, but though there were other officers in and out of the room, there were no further incidents."

I never heard of the outcome, nor was I really interested, other than the fact that I didn't wish to be brought in to any sort of enquiry, though I was a little disappointed in that I was unable to record the episode as one of the successes of the C.C.T.V. in my temporary charge.

In the years marked by the worldwide depression, the nineteen twenties and thirties, the police force advertised any vacancies which existed within their particular areas. A date and time for applicants to attend would bring dozens of men, who, through no fault of their own, were on the brink of destitution. There were none of the benefits which are currently available and it was common for former miners and such, to be prepared to walk many miles in the hope of landing a job. Some twenty or more would present themselves at the Manchester City Police Headquarters at the appointed hour, only to hear the recruiting officer announce that everyone who was under the height of six feet two inches, would not be required. There followed an elementary test of arithmetic and English and perhaps a medical inspection, then the vacancies, maybe for five constables would be filled and the remainder of the applicants told they would not be required.

Many of the officers who were appointed under those circumstances, were still serving when I joined. My height was five feet eleven and a half which I thought was reasonable, but whilst being shown round the division by one of the old coppers, I had serious thoughts of resigning.

We passed a couple of middle aged women and I heard one say to the other, "look at that little policeman."

I glanced at our reflections in a shop window and tended to agree with her. My colleague towered over me, at about six feet three and around twenty stone.

Over the next few years, as these old bobbies took their retirement and difficulty was experienced in the area of recruitment, the minimum height requirement plunged to five feet eight inches. Whenever any member of the public made reference to one of the lads, I would tell them that the officer had lied about his height.

Of course these days there is no need for an officer to be of excessive stature as they are not walking about on their own without means of contacting anyone. The arrest of some powerful raging drunk, about a mile from the station, required a physical advantage which was greater than that of the officer's adversary. Thankfully, present day officers, in vehicles, with radio contact, are in a position to obtain assistance.

Additionally, they are precluded from rendering a person who is bent on injuring the arresting officer, hors de combat, as any spectator, and the arrestee himself would expect. Some of the coppers who were preparing to retire as I joined, were legends, both among the men with whom they worked and the general public.

Alf Watson, known as Scarface, for reasons which were blatantly obvious, was one of the sergeants on my division and older people still speak of him to this day. An exceptionally large person, who struck fear in to most of the residents as he doled out his own punishment to wrongdoers. His sudden appearance at some nefarious activity such as a gambling school on a croft or open ground, would cause everyone present to scatter. He would throw his sergeant's stick with such expertise, as to bring a fleeing individual down as the three foot long piece of solid ebony, which he called his lie detector, passed between the runner's knees.

On retrieving his stick he would order the victim to go at once to the station and await him there. Very few failed to comply as they well knew he would come across them at some later date. It was said that he had a form of surgery, to which mothers would bring their wayward offspring. After the visit and a probable chastisement, he would tell the parent to "take him home, and if he's no better by weekend, bring him back!"

Luke Parker was another of the giants, an awesome figure, the son of a Lincolnshire farmer. It was rumoured that his father was distraught when he joined the police, as from being quite young, he could pull any of the various farm carts and the plough as good as any horse, and he didn't cost as much.   The Manchester force had a very good tug of war team, which had won lots of cups and trophies in the nineteen thirties, and big Luke was its anchor man.

On an occasion when the team were matched against the Royal Ulster Constabulary, both teams were relaxing on the night before the contest, in the club house. Over a couple of pints, the Manchester lads announced, good humouredly, that their anchor man could pull the Irish tem over on his own. He was taken up on it and in the middle of the moonlit playing field, he wrapped the rope around him, whilst the Ulstermen took up the strain and at a given signal began to pull. Luke, a cigarette dangling from the corner of his mouth, dug the heels of his size fifteen boots in to the turf and at an opportune moment, gave a mighty pull, at which the host team fell in a heap and were dragged along for several feet.

At the official contest the next day, the Irish boys, psychologically destroyed, were beaten three nil.

Those men are gone forever and would fail to fit in today. They wouldn't fit in to a police car anyway!

There were still plenty of the large lads about when I was getting close to retirement, not least Vincent Livesy, or 'Big Daddy' as he was better known. Vincent and I were promoted to sergeant around the same time, and as we were chatting one evening the landlord of a small local pub approached.

"There's a scrap in the vault," he announced, at which we followed him across the main road and in to his beer house. I turned in to the tiny vault where everyone was engaged in battle and began the process of imposing order.

Suddenly, the fighting ceased, and to my surprise, was replaced by roars of laughter from the now redundant combatants. I turned to see that 'Big Daddy' in an attempt to come to my aid, was jammed in the doorway to the room. He was unable either to get in or out of the aperture. Customers from the other room of the inn joined in pulling him back in to the corridor, whilst the former fighting men pushed from the vault side.

The combined efforts of the two factions resulted in the six feet two, twenty stone mass, leaving the portal like a cork from a bottle and joining me on the pavement outside.

"Don't let it happen again," he shouted at the group assembled in the corridor, and together we strolled off to our separate sections.

Chapter Six

There is something of an inevitability that the inexplicable would present itself when a large group of individuals, separately walk around in the lonely hours of the night. Strange situations have been the experience of sceptical, hard bitten men who have the skin of a rhinoceros and don't know what the word fear means.

There were of course one or two exceptions, and a perfect place to test that out was a municipal park land called Boggart Hole Clough. The old English word Boggart means ghost and that tells us that the area is supposedly haunted. There was a beat which was worked on a bicycle and it was necessary that the officer on that beat passed through the middle of the clough at least twice on each shift.

The experience was totally different in daylight, but at night there was an eerie strange air about the place. As you traversed the narrow lanes, shrouded by old trees which appeared to groan in the wind, you could swear that there were footfalls behind you and in the absence of illumination, the mind was tricked in to imagining that the Boggart was following you.

Access was gained to the clough by a narrow passage which left the nearby avenue of houses and descended, steeply in to the park. At the termination of the passage stood an old rain shelter, where on occasions, tramps could be found, sleeping off the effects of some cheap but effective alcohol. The lane taken in order to get through the clough and across to the next part of the beat, led from the shelter by way of a very steep incline. Here, most of us would find it necessary do dismount from the bike and push it to the top of the hill.

A young constable joined the section for his first tour of nights and was allocated the beat which required him to pass through the clough. Whilst waiting to given any jobs to be done on the various beats, the rest of the lads, for the benefit of the fresh officer, casually discussed the Boggart and invented a string of activities he was supposed to take part in. Due out on his beat, one of the officers sped to the clough and concealed himself in the crumbling shelter. When the new boy dismounted at the bottom of the passage, he let out the most awful howling and screeching. The constable leapt on to the bicycle, and leaving behind a shower of cinders, he pedalled at speed clear to the top of the hill and kept going until he reached the sanctuary of the well lit road at the exit to the park.

For the rest of the fortnight, he never entered the clough again, choosing instead, to cycle some two miles out of his way in order to avoid the consequences of being confronted by the Boggart. The lad survived for a further month, until nights came round again, and resigned.

When former inspector Dan Ewington was a young policeman, he became one of a number of other officers who have, for many years, been unable to explain a phenomenon which befell them around the Christmas period of nineteen sixty four.

"Something had taken place when it was my night off, which I was not aware of, as being a probationary constable, nobody ever told me anything," said Dan.

It transpired that police constable Alan Read, who was one of the motorcyclists on the division, was passing the main gates of Moston Cemetery at about one o'clock in the morning when he saw a little old woman there. She was wearing a bonnet and shawl and gave the appearance of a Victorian mill worker, as he had seen in many old photographs. It was a bitterly cold night, with an icy blast cutting along Moston Lane. He drove up to the old girl and asked her if she was all right. The woman ignored him, and fairly satisfied that everything was in order, he turned the bike round, and in doing so, looked over his shoulder to find she had disappeared.

He returned to the scene of his encounter, but there was no trace, so he dismounted and ascertaining that the cemetery gates were locked, the bemused officer drove away. The following night Dan was standing at the junction of Moston

Lane with Kenyon Lane about two o'clock, when another police motorcyclist, whom he didn't know, drove towards him from the direction of the cemetery, and drawing up alongside him, announced that he had seen the old lady, who was walking along the lane towards them.

"I jumped on to the pillion of the bike and we rode to Walter Street Police Station where the section sergeant, on hearing the motorcyclist's report, and being fully aware of Alan's experience of the previous night, was determined to get to the bottom of it." said Dan.

Everyone on the section was posted out strategically along Moston Lane and instructed not to interfere with the woman at that stage, but to inform the sergeant of anything which transpired.

"At about two fifteen, from a deep doorway, I saw the woman as she passed me. I watched her walk along for a few yards and then, realising she would have reached a point where she must have come in to the view of the next officer, I sprinted down the lane to join him," said Dan.

The CID office, Mill Street Police Station, 1960

"He said he had seen her approaching and that she just vanished before his eyes. Certainly she was nowhere about and could not have entered any of the shops which lined her route as they were all premises that were not lived on. A quick check revealed that all the padlocked doors were secure as I had seen them so, earlier," Dan added.

All the officers attended the station, where the sergeant held a briefing on the matter and a few minutes later, a telephone call was received from a man who lived in Factory Lane, the continuation of Moston Lane.

"That bloody Factory Lane ghost has been at it again. She's been rattling my back door and banging on the windows," he ranted.

The constable sent round by the sergeant, reported back that the phantom disturbance was something of a regular occurrence.

"He says he's reported it many a time over the ten years he's lived there, and that he was once told by his neighbours that it had been happening for at least the sixty years that he had lived on the street.

"I worked on the Walter Street section fairly regularly over the years and I have to say that I never saw the old girl. On the other hand, there were so many kind invitations to partake of the cup that cheers on nights, at Christmas that I may very well have wished her good night as we passed each other on many occasions."

My own experience in ghostly matters is limited to a wet night in Gorton, when, as a sergeant, I was walking along Hyde Road at midnight, along with a constable. There appeared a woman in night attire, who was travelling at top speed out of nearby Gladstone Street onto the main road before us, and a man who wearing nothing but a pair of underpants, was running behind her. The scene was common enough in the area, and the deduction that it was one of those husband and wife tiffs, where the woman was attempting to escape a Saturday night beating, the officer set off to intervene.

By the time I reached the little group it had become obvious that the incident was nothing of the sort. The constable said that the pair were in fact fleeing from a haunting., and the husband, though totally underdressed for such a night, stood barefooted whilst giving his explanation in the pouring rain.

"We were in bed and we both suddenly woke up, "began the shivering man.

"There was a grey figure in the corner of the bedroom, with very long arms and as he walked towards us, we both jumped out of bed and ran out, then you saw us," explained the female.

At first they both refused to return to their home, and I had difficulty in persuading them to do so. The woman insisted that I do not ask her to re-enter the house and when we arrived at the open door, she asked me to pass her some clothing out.

"The baby's in the bedroom sergeant," its father announced.

"Could you bring it down?," pleaded the mother.

I went up to the offending bedroom and sure enough, there was a the baby, blissfully unaware of the circumstances. There being no sign of a grey man, I carried the child downstairs and tucked it into its pram as requested. The couple, still on the pavement, had struggled in to the clothing which had been passed to them by the constable, and upon the receipt of their offspring, asked us to extinguished the lights and pull the door to, which I did.

"What are you going to do now?" I enquired.

" Going to my mother's at Droylsden," answered the mother.

I reminded them that it was all of six miles away and there were no buses, to no avail. There being nothing more to be done I left the officer to continue on his beat. Some time later, when on a morning shift, I called in a shop in the area, and knowing the lady there was a mine of information, I asked if she knew anything about the tenant on Gladstone Street whom we had assisted those weeks before.

"The haunted house you mean?" was her casual reply. "No they left you know; well nobody ever stays there for long anyway."

During the first moves which were destined to fill police buildings with unnecessary bureaucratic departments, the office which had for many years dealt with the statistical, records and efficiently run by one sergeant and two constables, was amongst the first to be reorganised. Larger accommodation was provided, and a new staff of a chief clerk, an assistant chief clerk and fourteen clerks was installed. The sergeant and his own staff were kept on for a short period, in order to acquaint the others with the filing systems he had instigated. When the civilian staff had settled in, the officers were sent back to their original divisions to work the three shifts, a duty which they had believed would not be carried out by them ever again.

One of the jobs which cropped up in the department from time to time was to furnish the Home Office with statistics which were required by the Home Secretary, in order that he would be in a position to answer questions in Parliament. Every police force in the land was involved, and in receipt of such a request, on a Friday afternoon usually, it was a case of all hands on deck in order to get them off on the midnight train to London in time for their collation and presentation on Monday morning.

On the first occasion that the new statistics clerks, at ten minutes to five on a Friday, were informed of the task by the superintendent, they were preparing themselves to be on their various modes of transport home.

"Sorry" said the chief clerk, "but we finish at five, as you know."

The superintendent, who had never met that problem when the department was handled by police officers, was unable to enforce the civilian staff to remain and work at getting whatever it was the Home Secretary required. Five minutes later, sitting in the deserted office, he had a brainwave, and rang the divisions the officers had been returned to. The sergeant was in bed, he being on nights, and the constables were out on their beats. In no time at all they were collected and transported to headquarters, where they set about a task they were well used to.

At midnight, the package safely on the train, they went home. That sergeant and the two constables went on to be brought in on numerous occasions over the ensuing years until the last of them retired, at which time, I suppose, they found an alternative. I was enjoying my twelve months in the vice squad, when the plain clothes sergeant instructed us all to come in on a Sunday.

"I've had a complaint that the gent's urinal on Ten Acres Lane is being used on Sundays as a meeting place for men who misbehave in there."

The offences he was referring to were of gross indecency between males in a public place. Not to go in to such fine a detail, suffice it to say, that although practices of that nature had recently been de-criminalized, following the Lord Wolfenden report, they may only be lawful when in private, between consenting males.

In these more enlightened times relationships of a gay nature are accepted by most people as being no business of theirs, but just as any heterosexual act taking place in a public place might cause offence to the onlooker and become a subject of complaint, the same applies, as you would expect, to any other liaison, In either case, as in all other official complaints made to the police, the matter must be looked in to and a satisfactory conclusion drawn.

Ten Acres Lane is some half a mile long, and the brick toilet building, on the edge of an expanse of playing fields, was isolated. Therefore I was surprised at ten o'clock on a Sunday morning, to find about twenty cars parked outside the convenience. The sergeant gave the order to enter the premises and as we did so we found the small area in the stalls crammed with men who were all carrying out acts of an indecent nature.

In all, on that first Sunday, there were ten men arrested, all of whom appeared at court on Monday and were convicted.

Before making our way to the toilets the following Sunday, the sergeant made the observation that we had been unable to detect anything taking place in the locked cubicles on the previous visit, but that he had noticed that there was a loft and that the entrance to it was through what had been a hatch at the pitch of the roof. He ordered one of the lads to climb in to the loft and to observe through the many holes in the ceiling.

"If you see any offences going on, come back to the hatch and wave your hanky," was his instruction. "We can then run in and arrest the offenders you have evidence on."

The chosen officer, being the smallest among us, was soon ensconced in the roof and lying down, was able to see every cubicle in the establishment. The cavalcade of vehicles had not yet put in an appearance, but as the constable's eyes became used to the darkness below, he saw that a large man in the clothing of a workman, was making use of the toilet immediately underneath him, in a completely lawful manner. The odour created from his quite natural offices was unbearable, and the officer scrambled out of the hatch as fast as he was able.

The sergeant misinterpreted his actions to mean that there was something illegal taking place and led the rest of us in a dash, culminating at the door of the cubicle, from which the big chap was emerging. The poor fellow was at first shaken by the sudden attention he was being given by the crowd who had burst in on him, and who, having experienced the loathsome aroma in the confined space, vanished as quickly as it had appeared, left the confines of the convenience and returned to his digging duties some yards away.

When the Sunday trippers began to drive up they found the rendezvous no longer attractive and sought an alternative well away from the area. The sergeant cancelled any further action with regard to the place, other than to recommend that the building be demolished, which in due course it was.

Still serving my twelve months in the department, there was concern voiced in higher circles, with regard to the many reports of a man who's habit it was to appear in a state of nakedness in various districts of the division.

"The boss wants to know why he hasn't been charged. About eighteen months he's been at it and he wants him locked up," said the sergeant.

The trouble with that kind of offender is that, unless the police actually come across them in the act, or their victim knows who they are, there is little chance of apprehension and they are well aware of it. As in lots of cases a lucky break is the answer and ours came quite by chance one evening when I was given an enquiry under the auspices of the Post Office. It was the duty of that organisation to inform us of anything that they considered to be of an obscene nature, which was being sent through the post, and I was handed the opened package by the sergeant.

"Go and see whoever sent for this lot," he directed.

The address was in the area of Crumpsall and turned out to be a semi-detached house in a fairly good class part of the district. My knock brought a tall man of some forty years to the door, and when I introduced myself, he asked me in to a small room which led off the hall. His wife entered the room, a woman whom I would describe as being of perfectly respectable appearance, and as I didn't wish her to be upset by my visit, I told her that I was there to speak to her husband with regard to his having witnessed an accident.

When she left us I broached the subject of the contents of the packet addressed to him, which he admitted having sent for and when I showed him the contents he explained that his interest in the images were of a purely academic nature. The pictures, all of women in various poses and without clothing, some entertaining male companions, also devoid of modesty, were studied by the recipient.

"I am very interested in the human form," he said.

I had a sudden thought from nowhere, and looking him straight in the eye I said.

"I know you are interested, because you have been displaying your own naked body to women all over the place for a long time.

Now get your coat because we're going to the station to sort it all out."

The man seemed to age before my eyes and begged me not to disclose the reason for his going with me. He called his wife to the room and told her he was going to see photographs in an effort to identify a driver.

She smiled sweetly and was joined by a small boy, to whom she explained that daddy was helping a policeman to catch a naughty man and would be back shortly. At the station he confessed to having exposed himself so many times over the last couple of years that he couldn't remember precisely where or when. I charged him with some which had been reported and managed to get him in court on a Saturday morning, when the press were absent. The magistrates ordered probation and recommended some form of treatment, which may well have worked, as there were no further sightings of the phantom nudist. I hope that his family never discovered the true circumstances of my couple of hours with the breadwinner and lived happily ever after.

The printing of newspapers used to be labour intensive and much of the work was carried out overnight. Around one or two o'clock in the morning the staff would take their break and invariably repair to a nearby pub. Of course, should the licensee be foolish enough to supply them with intoxicating liquor at that hour of the morning, he would be breaking the law, and those who chanced being caught took elaborate steps to avoid the police gathering evidence of their wrong doing.

Once their late night customers were on the premises there would be the minimum of illumination and there would be the rule of no raised voices. The secret knock, in order that only newspaper men could gain entrance, was changed nightly and could be found written in chalk on the inside of the staff exit a few minutes before the bell for break time was sounded.

The police were not really interested in these nightly rituals, as of course there was never any of the nuisances which occur during the permitted hours, the newsmen merely knocking back as much as they could in the short time that the break facilitated and quietly walking back from the pub to their printing duties.

As in most cases the prosecution of pubs and clubs arose from complaints made by the public, or often by irate partners, and it was from such a source that my colleague Joe and myself were directed to investigate licensed premises which lay in close proximity to the *News Chronicle* printing establishment.

We noticed that the work force wore blue boiler suits and our first step was to acquire identical overalls from the stores. We donned the disguise and positioned ourselves in the close proximity of the exit door just before one o'clock and when the lads began to trickle out, I popped inside to look what the code was. Once I had the three numbers I joined Joe and we waited to join the stragglers in the short walk to the pub. On arrival at the door of the hostelry, I tapped out the code on the window and, according to custom, the last man in opened up for us. In the darkened bar there were some thirty men, all dressed as we were, and all guzzling beer, whilst conversing in hushed tones.

"What time's your lift?" asked the man who made room for us on a form. I had no idea what he was talking about, and for a moment I hesitated.

Joe stepped in and said, "He's a bit deaf, got blown up in Italy."

Another man leaned across and shouted in to my ear that he had been wounded at Casino, whilst another having landed in France on D-Day, good naturedly referred to us as D-Day Dodgers. There was some further banter which brought the end of the break period and we all surreptitiously slipped out of the pub, and with the exception of just two, went back to work.

On the way to the station, Joe, who had been a fighter pilot, pointed out that the lads we had been drinking with deserved to relax for half an hour, and the following lunchtime we called in the pub and advised him to tell his late night clientele he was going to bed early for a week. There were no further complaints respecting the beer house so Joe and I handed back our overalls to the stores and concentrated on important other matters.

Close by one of the section stations stood an old established family butcher's shop, where the proprietor, a third generation owner, carried out his trade to the satisfaction of his many loyal customers. The rationing of food which had been imposed by serious shortages during World War Two, were still in force up to some three or four years after the guns fell silent, and though some commodities like sweets and chocolates were still rationed until nineteen fifty three, the meat trade was back to normal.

One or two unscrupulous butchers had been able to provide people with unlimited supplies of meat all through the war, at an inflated price of course, and without the requirement of a ration book. It became obvious to me that those butchers believed the police were aware of all that, when in fact they were probably not, but a commodity which had never been rationed, sausages, could be purchased by officers for sixpence (two and a half pence today) a pound in weight, a practice still going on well into the nineteen fifties.

A complaint was made by a local woman whom I went to see at her home which was nearby to the old family butcher's shop. The lady, like most of her contemporaries, didn't beat around the bush.

"I went in to the butcher's, Sam's, on the corner, this morning to buy some sausages for my husband's tea, and you know how they lay 'em out on them flat trays? Well he brought the full tray round the counter to show me and asked me if they was all right. I said they seemed OK, then he got hold of my hand and started to press it down on the pile of sausages."

She hesitated for a moment and then sat down on a kitchen chair to gather her composure.

"I suddenly realised that one of his prime pork sausages was different from the rest," she said.

I asked her what she meant and she told me, in her own terms, that it was a part of Sam's anatomy. The woman had been clearly shocked, not to mention offended by what had taken place, and I popped round to see her tormentor.

He admitted that he had done as the complainant had told me and I took him in to the nearby section station. There were four constables there, having their breakfasts and at least two of them were chewing away at fried sausages which they had purchased from the inventive flasher.

"What you doing in here?" one of the lads enquired of the hapless trader. I told him in some detail what he was doing in there, and it was only the timely arrival of the vehicle which was to take us to headquarters, that stopped the diners from making mince-meat of him!

Chapter Seven

In the first decade of my police service, there occurred a significant change in the social life of those who resided in the Manchester City Police area of jurisdiction.

Prior to nineteen fifty three, and probably from the very beginning of the industrial revolution, the men, who sweated all day in the factories, as well as some of the women, left the factory gates and made straight for the nearest beer houses. Many housewives, who would also have been slaving all day with endless washing, ironing, cooking, not to mention looking after their numerous offspring, could never be certain that their thirsty husbands would be home for tea, or in time for bed.

On Fridays, if they were not at the factory gates as their lords and masters came out with their meagre wages, they might well discover the much needed cash had been spent on drink by the time he reached home. This was the stuff of domestic disputes, to which the man on the beat was often called.

Once the officer was inside the house, the wife would rant and rave at her wayward husband, bringing up things from the past that he had long forgotten, and goading the poor chap, in the knowledge that he was fairly unlikely to clout her whilst the constable was there. Occasionally, the tired and emotional spouse would become so fed up with scathing remarks from his beloved that he would be unable to bear any more, and fetch her a flat hander round the ear.

That, to the lady's satisfaction, would result in either her husband receiving a similar blow from the officer, though of a much harder velocity, or in the event of any attempt at retaliation, the errant man of the house being taken off to the station for the night. The trouble with the latter remedy was that the wife, in an attempt to regain some marital bliss, would appear at court the following day to speak up on her husband's behalf, usually explaining to the magistrates that she had sent for the officer so that he would merely advise her, and not to knock her man about and then lock him up.

All this became revealed to me on the first occasion when I dealt with a domestic in a similar way. Ever after, when called to a row of that nature, I would knock on the door and stand well back. When the woman opened the door I would ask about the circumstances then advise the services of a solicitor before strolling away.

Much of these troubles were of course due to drink. The social change I mentioned was nothing to do with governments, religions or the price of intoxicating liquor, it was the advent of television in the home, a luxury only available to the wealthy until someone made the sets easy to rent.

I have seen small groups of people crowded around the window of their local T.V. shop on a freezing night, watching a tiny screen on which someone worked away interminably in the process of producing a clay pot on a wheel. They might have gone on enjoying the only way they had of viewing for many more years, had it not been for the planned coronation of Her Majesty Queen Elizabeth The Second.

The announcement to the effect that the whole of the ceremony was to be presented on television, brought hundreds of customers to the various outlets where rental agreements were entered into, involving little more than a pound a week. As the homes of those workers who had hitherto made for the pub began to show films and variety shows in the front room, husbands hurried out of the factory gates and, ignoring the pubs, went straight home. By the time the coronation came, wives had already persuaded their men folk that the coins which jangled in their pockets, due to not being handed over to a publican, would come in useful for a new set of curtains or a carpet to replace the worn out linoleum.

Of course there were those men who were thankfully not seduced away from their quota of strong drink, nor from their unreasonable treatment of home and family, so that we were not deprived of the odd offender here and there. There came a noticeable change as the years went by, as parliament weakened the gravity of beer, which resulted in fewer men being found almost unconscious through drink, and lying on the pavement, or sometimes on the road.

By the nineteen seventies the pubs were empty during the week, save for those whose habit it was to turn up in the bar a quarter of an hour before last orders. At weekend it was another story, the difference being that husbands and wives were to be found together in pubs, and the sawdust strewn floors were gone, to be replaced by carpets, as seen in the television advertisements.

Public houses and the police went together like parsons and churches. The uniform branch finding the hospitality available during the night shift, a great comfort, and the C.I.D. finding a similar hospitality at any time, not merely a comfort but additionally a major source of information regarding nefarious activity on their particular patch.

I was never attracted to drinking in the daytime, whether on duty or otherwise, and on only one occasion did I make an exception. An abnormally hot and sticky Saturday lunchtime in August found me patrolling a beat in Blackley and at around one o'clock as I ambled past one of the small pubs, the licensee was standing at the entrance.

"You look hot constable. Bet you could go a pint?" he said.

I nodded in agreement, as the closed neck tunic I was wearing was really made for the winter, and though I wore nothing underneath it nevertheless was boiling hot, the tight collar having the effect of holding the hot air against my skin.

I followed him in to the premises and was a little surprised to find there were no customers there. It was the lunchtime break for many of the people employed at a huge chemical works and a wire manufacturers close by, and I had, a little while previously, seen throngs of them entering the several other pubs about. The kindly landlord pulled a pint of bitter which he handed to me, and I noticed that the customary foam at the top was absent. The taproom however was many degrees cooler than the exterior of the premises, and it was with gusto that I poured the contents of the glass down my throat. A little short of completely draining the vessel, a sort of heartburn sensation welled up in my gullet and I felt exceedingly nauseated.

"Another?" asked mine host, to which I made no reply, other than to wave to him as I quickly left for the street. I made my way with all speed to the haven of the nearby Tram Office, where a few of the drivers and conductors were taking their break.

"Hello Woody," one or two of them called as I shot past them and in to the toilets. I was violently sick, and grateful to have made it there without embarrassing my uniform in view of the public. After a short while I had recovered sufficiently enough to strike out up the steep hill to the section station, where I was sick again.

Ten minutes later, the shift was signed off and I wearily cycled home.

The ale I had consumed in the little inn was that of a Manchester family brewery, of which there were many at that time. I mentioned the incident to my father some time later, and he, being a connoisseur, informed me that the particular brew in question was delivered to the pubs in barrels, which when installed in the cellar required the publican to pour in a product of fish meal called finings. The finings gradually flowed to the bottom of the cask, taking down with it, any impurities.

"You obviously swallowed a load of fish meal before it had chance to reach the bottom of the barrel," he laughed.

The brewery has many smart pubs around to this day, but I have never been able to enter any of them, even though I am assured that the finings practice is a thing of the past.

Since the disappearance of the beat man on foot, and the progression to the coverage by cops in cars, the old alliance between Mr. Beer house and Mr. Plod has fallen in to disuse. The C.I.D. continue to prop up the bar, albeit in order to conduct a genuine enquiry, and with the sanction of a senior officer.

In the past, it was common, when a uniform officer was selected to become a detective, for the superintendent to have a chat with the candidate's wife. That lady would be told that should her husband be transferred, she may expect to see very little of him, and that whenever she did he would no doubt have been drinking. Clock watchers in the C.I.D. were not tolerated, nor were teetotallers.

When I became the Plain Clothes Sergeant, I decided to forget the old animosity and formed an immediate liaison with the detective branch, a liaison which fell at the fence when I was asked to raid a pub on their behalf.

"The place is being used for the selling of stolen property," said one of the detective sergeants, "and the licensee refuses to cooperate with us whenever we suspect one or other of the toe rags who booze in the place. He serves 'em till all hours, specially on Saturday nights."

The premises, he told me, were the Lock Gates Tavern, down by the canal, and on the ensuing Saturday, at midnight, together with my team of plain clothes officers, I entered the place. Sure enough, the rooms were packed with customers who were drinking merrily away and the licensee was happily filling the trays with which the army of waiters miraculously balanced pints of beer as they weaved through the crowded tables. I pushed through to the bar and introduced myself.

"Seven pints is it ?" yelled the landlord, who, when I declined and announced the purpose of the visit, immediately shut down the bar. My team were busy entering the particulars of the illegal drinkers and when the howling mob were off the premises, I informed the publican that he was to be prosecuted.

On Monday, when I entered the C.I.D. Office, I experienced a distinct atmosphere of discontent towards myself which prevailed throughout the morning and it was lunchtime before I discovered the reason for it. The sergeant who had made the request regarding the Lock Gates Tavern, approached me in the canteen.

"There's the Lock Gates Tavern, and there's the Lock Gates Inn," he said. " You did the bloody Inn which is the C.I.D. watering hole, the one I asked you to do is a couple of miles further along the canal, the bloody Tavern!"

By the time I was transferred to the C.I.D. some months later, the affair had blown over, and the wayward landlord of the Tavern had been dealt with under the Ways and Means Act.

Amongst the many industries on the division was a large and important coal mining operation. Thousands of hard working men toiled a couple of miles below ground on shifts and at certain times of the day the district was flooded with them as they came and went. I always held an admiration for those lads, knowing that they had a job which I could never do. Indeed, the reason for my volunteering for the army at the age of seventeen was to avoid the pits.

As I waited eagerly to be called up for the forces at eighteen, I had a friend, who when he reached that age, was called up to work in the mines at Yorkshire.

"They call us the Bevin Boys," he said. "Out of every hundred lads who register for conscription, three are sent down the mines."

Upon hearing that news, I was down at the recruiting office the following morning where I volunteered for what was termed the duration of emergency and a couple of months later I was safely in khaki and mainly above ground.

There were occasions when police officers were obliged to go down to the coal face, as there were numerous fatal accidents there which had to be investigated on behalf of the coroner, and a lot of officers were taken down when they expressed a curiosity to see what it was like. One such constable strolled on to the pit just before the cage was about to take the miners down, and was invited aboard. At the bottom of the shaft, instead of remaining in the cage and going back up he joined the colliers as they stepped off into the pit.

The cage, filled with men who had completed their shift, shot away to the surface and the officer was stranded. Up above, when the sergeant visited the spot where the officer should have put in an appearance at four thirty, he impatiently banged his stick on the pavement. For ten minutes, the metal tip of his badge of office rang persistently upon the stone flags of the footpath, in due course, bringing the officer from the adjoining beat in answer.

"Have you seen anything of two sixteen?" asked the sergeant. The officer's negative reply sent the sergeant striding to the station. There being no indication of the missing man being engaged with anything, the inspector was informed and he attended at the constable's next point at five fifteen.

In the bowels of the earth, two sixteen, having been informed that he would be unable to surface before eleven fifteen that evening, sat despondently on an upturned box. The heat was almost unbearable, and even the comfort of a cigarette was strictly forbidden. The inspector had organised a search of the missing officer's beat, which involved all the other officers on the section, and at eleven o'clock, when they went off, the night staff took it up.

Around eleven thirty there appeared, in the charge office, an apparition in a helmet, whoss uniform face and hands were blackened by layers of coal dust. The search was called off and a while later he was before the Deputy Chief Constable. He had no other recourse than to honestly explain what had happened, and the deputy chief, having been an operational policeman himself for many years, took a lenient view of it and fined him twenty pounds. He added the instruction that he was not to do it again, and two sixteen never did.

The probationer constable, in his second week in the job, walked in to the small section station in order to hand in a piece of found property which had been given to him by a member of the public. The station officer, a constable of many years service was in the back yard, where in an effort to relieve the boredom of a Sunday morning, he was hosing down a batch of grappling irons, kept normally in a shed there. In reply to the young lad's query, he informed him jokingly that every Sunday, the whole of the section had to carry out grappling drill down at the canal and when the drill was over, it was the station officer's job to wash the equipment before putting it away in preparation for the next Sunday morning.

"You should have been on the practice. Weren't you told?" kidded the older man. The probationer said that he was not and the station officer told him, if asked, to say that he had attended the practice.

"What's it for anyway?" asked the lad.

"So that we can get drowned people out of the water of course," hissed his tormentor.

The young constable left the station, and as he did so he came face to face with the chief superintendent who was on his way in. He saluted and he was asked what he was doing.

"I've been on grappling iron drill sir," he replied smartly. The chief superintendent was newly appointed, indeed it was his first Sunday morning inspection of the stations and he asked the officer what form the drill took. The probationer gave a full explanation of the methods employed in order to retrieve bodies from the canal, which suitably impressed his superior officer. On the following day he chaired a meeting of his superintendents, chief inspectors and inspectors, during which he brought up the matter of the grappling iron practice.

As he spoke at length on the subject he detected blank looks before him.

"You do know about the practice don't you?" he enquired bad temperedly.

It became apparent that they had no idea of what he was talking about, and the chief superintendent, nicknamed 'Fiery Bob', throughout his service, yelled that they were to get out on the division and find out whether there was anything else going on that they didn't know about.

Having been away from the training centre for eight years, and having no pressing desire to return, I was surprised when the divisional administration inspector informed me that, as the physical training instructor there had broken his leg, I was to replace him until such time as he was fit enough to return.

"How did you know I'd been a P.T.I. In the army?" I asked.

"It's on your record file," he replied.

Protestation on my part fell upon stony ground, and all attempts to point out that the degree of physical fitness required in order to instruct others, had to be at the highest of levels, far above my own, which after some ten years of comparative inactivity was far from being satisfactory.

The inspector pointed out that the more such duties appeared on the records, the greater the chance of promotion to sergeant in the future, to which I agreed to do as I had been asked. The following Monday I turned up at the Northwest District Police Training Centre, complete with track suit and pumps, salvaged from the days when I was responsible for loosening the sinews of young soldiers, in order that they became fighting fit and fit to fight.

"There are two periods of P.T. each day," explained the Camp Commandant as we strolled towards the gymnasium. "And on Mondays I like every student to take part in a five mile run and walk, straight after breakfast. Gets the weekend out of their system you know."

There was a small room with a bed, a table and two chairs, which was to be all mine for the next few months, where, as the commandant left me to unpack, he said the five mile jaunt, having been cancelled earlier, would take place in an hour. I hurriedly unpacked, donning the track suit and pumps, then after a quick survey of the gym, set out for the parade square. The recruits both men and women in P.T. kit began to assemble until some hundred or more were there.

The drill sergeant, a no nonsense former Welsh Guardsman, arrived and formed everyone in to three ranks then immediately retired to the sergeant's mess.

I gave the order "right turn" then led the column out through the main gates and on to the road at a jog. I had been advised that twice round the perimiter of the training centre was approximately five miles and after a couple of hundred yards, when my legs began to give way, and my lungs started to protest, I ordered the students to change to marching. During the remainder of the exercise, I made two more attempts at the double which I quickly altered to marching again in sympathy with my aching limbs and clapped out lungs.

By the following Monday I had made some progress in adapting to the taxing programme, and a fortnight later I was practically fit.

Most of my free time was spent in the gymnasium, where I made full use of the splendid apparatus provided. I conducted the classes with the trainees, strictly in accordance with the procedures for the training of army personnel in their first three months, which has the effect of gradually reaching a very high standard that is easy to maintain.

Eventually the regular instructor returned and I was back on the beat. There were no facilities in the force for officers to continue in keeping fit programmes, nor was there any encouragement to do so. By the end of their service most policemen would have gained at least four stones in weight, and that was when they were on walking beats.

Police constable Bill (chunky) Collins, who's hobby was weight training, discussed with me the feasibility of starting a weight training club at the divisional headquarters and the permission of the chief superintendent was granted. He allocated a disused room in the cellar and those officers showing a willingness to join cheerfully handed over half a crown each with which to buy weightlifting equipment.

There were around twenty five eager coppers at the first session. Bill demonstrated the correct methods of using the weights and we both insisted that everyone keep strictly to his rule of starting off with light loads and building up over weeks until the muscles had adapted, then adding a few more pounds to the bar and so on. We related to our members the origins of the sport, that of a farmer in ancient Greece, who, on finding a calf had been born lame, hoisted it on to his shoulders each morning to take it to the meadow, and carried it back to the stall in the evening.

Within a year the animal had grown to full size and the farmer was surprised to discover that he was able to carry it with no more effort than when it was small. He himself had grown in stature and sported the perfectly chiselled frame of a Greek god.

At that explanation, the lads set about the equipment with enthusiasm but in an effort to bypass a slow lead up as Bill advised, they set about filling the bars with excessive weight, and finding that for the next couple of days their muscles ached far too much for them to continue, the membership dwindled to just me and Bill.

The two of us continued to make use of the abandoned equipment for a number of years benefitting greatly from the extra strength it gave.

Most nicknames were awarded early in the recipient's service and stayed with him until the end of his days. Police constable Arthur Davenport earned his, 'Sparkler' in his first few months on the beat. He was working from a section station which covered one of the busiest districts of the division, and whilst in there to take his refreshments, the station officer had occasion to ask him how many summonses he had submitted since joining. Arthur said that the grand total was none!

There were so many different coloured forms in connection with the application for summonses, and such a complicated confusion involved not least the terrifying experience of having to stand in front of the chief superintendent whilst explaining the circumstances It was far easier to feel someone's collar, and that's what he frequently did.

"Well," barked the station officer. "I expect you to submit a summons application before you go off duty today!"

Had Arthur had the audacity to enquire from his mentor as to the total of such applications he had submitted over the past twenty years he would have found the answer to compare very closely with that of his own.

A determination, however, to take the plunge, drew his attention to the approach of two young children walking towards him, both of whom were carrying fireworks. He stopped the pair, a girl aged ten and a lad aged four.

"Where did you get those from?" he asked.

"From the shop up there," said the girl, her voice trembling as she pointed back up the road.

"When did you buy them?" he demanded.

"A minute ago sir," replied the girl.

Arthur took the kids back to the shop, one of those establishments to be found everywhere in those days in which anything could be purchased from aspirins to bottles of beer; a general store in fact.

There was a queue of five people waiting to be served by the ageing proprietor, and the officer joined the end of the line with the offending children. When his turn came, he asked the woman whether she had sold the fireworks to the kids, to which she replied that she had.

"Don't you realise that the selling of fireworks to anyone under thirteen is an offence?" Arthur asked.

"No, not really," answered the old girl, wiping her hands on a grubby apron.

He took the children home and continued to the station for his dinner. The station officer, poking his head around the door of the dining room, enquired as to whether he had a summons to apply for.

"What is it?" he asked. "Piracy on the high seas or conspiracy to overthrow the government?"

"Fireworks sold to children," replied Arthur.

"Did you examine her Gunpowder Licence?" asked one of the other constables present. At first he thought it was a wind up, but when the enquirer brought a book in from the office, in which the requirement was clearly outlined, he set off to once again to confront the irate shopkeeper.

To the annoyance of several women waiting to be served, she shuffled off into her private quarters in search of the licence. One of the women asked him whether or not he had caught any burglars lately, which inspired a general conversation with regard to the persecution of innocent children.

After what seemed to Arthur to be an eternity, she emerged waving an ancient piece of yellowed parchment upon which was scrawled the particulars of her permission to sell fireworks. The reference to the many restrictions were unclear, as at some time in the distant past, a cup of tea had apparently been spilled over it. When constable Davenport returned the station officer was on the telephone.

On seeing Arthur he said to the caller: "Oh yes, Sparkler's just walked in!"

If at any gathering of old retired policemen, there is a reference made to P.C. B 8 Davenport, many present will not know who that is. But if you say 'Sparkler', they will all know.

Chapter Eight

"Nobody ever got the better of me," said the old burglar, as I joined him at the bar of the Crown one Saturday evening.

He was one of the old school, almost a gentleman, who would no more think of attacking his victims than going teetotal.

" 'Cept for two people that is. The wife, and that was before we was married. Two nights afterwards, while I was asleep, she found a fish hook in my trouser pocket, and after that I could have left a hundred pounds there. It spoilt what some people call a honeymoon, but it paid off in the long run."

I enquired as to the identity of the other person who had apparently outwitted him, and his answer came with a loud and drawn out sigh.

"Detective Sergeant Howard Norman, that's who," he said.

I knew the sergeant he was referring to as a master of eccentricity, and would not be surprised as to whatever it was that had upset my companion.

"It must have been about twelve years ago. I had been asked by a neighbour to get him one of the new television cassette recorders from the T.V. shop on the main road, and around one in the morning I smashed the glass out of the front door, grabbed the recorder and set off with it under my arm. What I didn't know, was that a young copper had heard the glass go and was now running towards me. I set off through the side roads and back entries with him some distance behind me.

"As you know I used to live in Caesar Street, that small street at the back of the police station, and as I pelted down there I could hear the copper's running footsteps coming along the back entry. Well I reached the front door of our house and was inside before he turned in to the street. All the neighbours were asleep, so all the houses including ours were in darkness, though he obviously heard me slam the front door. I watched him tiptoe up and down, listening at every one of the twenty four doors, and in the end, he gave up, so I went to bed." he related.

I asked where the D.S. came in, and he told me that the disappointed officer, on going in to the station to report the break in, had run in to Howard at the front door. The sergeant then apparently gathered two or three uniformed men and took them round to Caesar Street.

"I was looking out of the window as he came in to the street, and I quickly got undressed and popped in to bed. I heard him telling the others to get everyone in the street outside, which is what they did. I went downstairs and opened the front door, which a big copper had nearly battered down. He took me to the end of the street and pushed me in to a pile of neighbours who were already gathered there.

"It was a chilly night and everyone was in some sort of sleeping clothes, most of 'em in their bare feet. The D.S. sent the very young and the very old back in their houses, then marched the rest of us to the station."

I ordered us both another pint and asked about the stolen property.

"I just had time to dump it in the old woman's dustbin next door," he explained.

"What happened at the station?" I asked.

"Well he took us all, about thirty odd, down a long and freezing cell corridor and announced that as soon as the one he was looking for confessed to the break in and theft of the cassette recorder, the rest could go and get back in bed."

"How long did you stick it out for?" I asked.

"Just a few minutes," he said.

He went on to tell me that as they stood there, in various states of undress, particularly without shoes and socks on the concrete floor of the cell corridor, all eyes were turned on him. He stepped forward and told the sergeant that he was the guilty one, and that he was more than willing to assist in the matter, and to produce the stolen item.

Detective Sergeant Norman, true to his word, herded the rest of Caesar Street out of the station and back to their humble dwellings.

"I got eighteen months for that lot," said the hapless thief. " Mind you, I was glad in a way as they had all more or less calmed down by the time I got back home."

The same detective sergeant, some years later, had gone to a pub in the location of the docks and had struck up a friendship with a Russian sea captain there. After some hours of struggling with the sea dog's limitations in respect of the English language, made seemingly easier after the consumption of endless glasses of vodka, Howard accepted an invitation to join the captain aboard his vessel. In the state room, more of the cup that cheers was produced, during which time Howard detected a distinct motion of the ship. Through a series of hand signals he discovered that they were under way and well in to the River Mersey. He somehow was able to convince his host that he had no plans to visit the Soviet Union, and when the pilot came alongside to take the ship over the Bar, arrangements were made for him to transfer and be taken to Liverpool. Somehow he managed to get back to the office and then to his home, and the next day, fresh and breezy, he was back to almost normal.

Some years after I had retired and was employed by a department store, I was talking to another employee, who turned out to be the nephew of Howard. He told me that he had visited his uncle, who was by then the licensee of a village pub in Shropshire. He was well aware of his uncle's eccentricity, but none the less was surprised to find him serving his customers in the full uniform of a German officer, complete with swastika armband.

The customers apparently saw nothing untoward as they were used to seeing him in various costumes over the period of his colourful tenancy.

"The first evening he invited me and my mother, who was his sister, to a posh restaurant a couple of miles away, and I overheard him booking the table in the name of Mr. Silver," said my colleague. "My mother and I were in the bar when a taxi arrived and I called up the stairs to let uncle Howard know. When he came down, everyone burst in to laughter. He was dressed as Long John Silver, complete with stuffed parrot and a peg leg!"

The nephew went on to describe their arrival at the restaurant, where Howard, leaning on his crutch, bellowed that he was coming aboard.

"Mum and I were embarrassed, to say the least, and horrified to see that the table he had booked was in the centre of the room. Throughout the meal, he kept bawling and shouting about the treasure which had been stolen from him, and enquiring from individuals as to whether the had seen anything of Ben Gun."

From time to time, other retired officers have visited Howard at his little inn and have reported having seen him as the Town

Crier, a bishop and the Duke of Wellington!

Around nineteen seventy, I began to see a changing Britain. It was a time of shoulder length hair and big moustaches, of flared trousers and funny fags. The 'Love Thy Local Criminal' movement had well set in, and it seemed disrespectful for a law abiding citizen to criticise someone who had broken in to his home and stolen all his worldly goods, or who had viscously violated his women folk.

"They do it because they had their teddy bear taken off 'em when they were young," explained a colleague, sarcastically.

I could see that the disappearance of discipline from school and home would lead to unlawfulness on an unprecedented scale. The suffocating political correctness farce had not begun to raise its ugly head, and those of us who had spent our youth in a war to defend, amongst other things, freedom of speech, had not yet realised that they had buried their young friends in far off lands for nothing.

I was looking in to a serious matter of wounding, when these trends were in their infancy. A young man entered a chip shop on a Friday evening, and not realising that another youth, also in the shop, was waiting to be served, asked for a portion of chips. What he got instead was the blade of a knife thrust in to his back, which punctured a lung.

I soon had the perpetrator identified, and a couple of days later went to a block of council flats in the area. The lad I was after belonged to a notorious family, none of whom had ever been gainfully employed, preferring to accept state handouts, and stealing anything they required. I had another officer with me as I knew they would take exception to my visit.

I turned my back to the door of the flat and gave it a kick. The door flew open and we were inside. To our surprise the place was empty, and at seven in the morning that was most unusual as of course no one needed to be up for work. As we were leaving, a woman came to the door of her flat and told us that the whole six of them had gone on holiday for a fortnight.

"The Town Hall has sent 'em to Spain," she announced. "Went yesterday, next door's going when they come back, then the rest of the flats later on and ..."

I was on my way to the Town Hall before she could finish. There I was directed to an office in which sat the man responsible for the orgy of holidays on the rates. He was all hair and beads and very hostile.

"They are a deprived family and entitled to an annual holiday," he began to tell me.

I requested the address of the hotel and the precise date of their return.

"I won't tell you," he sneered.

I told him why I wished to know and that if he didn't tell me I would arrest him. At that he furnished me with all the particulars and I left him seething, though not before asking him if he could send my family on a free holiday to Spain.

"I've been saving up to go to North Wales for weeks," I explained. He made no reply.

The Police Convalescence Home at Harrogate in Yorkshire, is a place, as the name suggests, where the sick and injured members of the force can relax for a couple of weeks. Sometime, in the early fifties, whilst two Manchester officers were staying there, they met a sergeant who was in the police in North Wales. The sergeant was recovering from a minor operation and the Manchester consta-

A constable on duty at the corner of Market Street and Cross Street, early 20th century. Note his great height against those of pedestrians

bles, noticing that nobody seemed to have anything to do with him, took him under their wing, as it were.

When the sergeant returned to his little police station at Nefyn, he wrote to the chief constable of Manchester, pointing out the kindness shown by the two officers, and outlining that he was the owner of a cottage in the town. He went on to write, that any officer in Manchester would be welcome to occupy the cottage whilst on leave, for the favourable sum of ten shillings a week (50p). Needless to say, he was inundated with bookings, so much so that he persuaded others of his neighbours to provide similar accommodation, some of them going so far as to move in to their garages for the summer months, making all the facilities of their homes available as self catering establishments.

Of course, it was only he who was charging such a low price, the others were as much as £5 a week. Within a couple of years the area had become so well established throughout the force that it became a similar situation as the old Wakes Weeks, common to Lancashire mill towns, where the populations of places such as Oldham for instance, could be found wandering around in Blackpool. In other words, you were unable to walk more than a couple of yards without meeting a neighbour or work mate.

My own family holidayed at Nefyn on a number of occasions, taking full advantage of the sergeant's offer. A walk from the accommodation soon brought us, via a steep track to the beach, where another ten minutes trudge along the sands had to be negotiated in order to reach a high wall, giving shelter from the prevailing wind. The wall was in fact part of a jetty which was built in the middle of the nineteenth century to facilitate the Isle Of Man Steam Packet, and was abandoned as such after only a few months.

If, after the journey over the sands, you felt energetic enough to scale the steps of the jetty and down the other side, you would discover the old stone buildings, originally the offices etc., of the original project, which were now a gift shop and a quaint little fishermen's pub. All along the landside were steep high cliffs, which prompted me to enquire from the landlord as to how he had his barrels delivered.

"There's a couple of stanchions up at the top, and they lower everything down from there with ropes," he told me.

Never having been a daytime drinker, I never went over the wall again, preferring to stay on the beach and swimming in the sea.

In later years, as a sergeant, I was in the station when sergeant Tommy O'Donnell, whom I was about to take over from, came in. He had only returned from his first holiday in Nefyn that very morning and I asked whether or not he had enjoyed it.

"All right," he muttered dispiritedly.

I detected a note of discontent and asked for an explanation.

"You know that I love a couple of pints at dinner time, especially on holiday," he began. I and a couple of constables who were present, nodded in assent. "Well after struggling up the beach like a beast of burden with all the kid's things and parcels of sandwiches, we sat against a big high wall that used to be the jetty. Then I had to walk back half a mile, up the sloping road and all the way back in to Nefyn to get a pint or two.

"By the time I got back to the wife and kids, it was nearly time to go back to the digs for tea. She was moaning about it and the kids were eating ice cream cones. I asked them where they had got them from and the wife glared at them so hard, they got up and walked along the sands. We followed and at long last reached the cottage we were staying at."

He went on to explain that in order to keep the peace, he promised he would refrain from returning to the pub throughout the remainder of the stay.

"Why didn't you use the pub over the wall?" I asked.

"What pub, there's no pub there," he scoffed.

I told him of the inn that I found on the other side of the wall. "It's called the Cock," I said.

The name convinced him that I was making it up, and he told me so. At that moment, in came P.C. Jim Cooper, an officer who had spent more holidays at Nefyn than anyone.

"Where could I find a fully functioning pub on the beach at Nefyn? I asked. Jim immediately gave the exact location and name of the establishment.

"Up the steps and down the other side. Good drop of ale there. They have to lower the barrels down the cliffs you know," he said.

Tommy gazed towards the ceiling, and I could see from the twitching of his jaw that he was convinced as to the authenticity of my description of the close proximity of the Cock.

"You're right," he said, through gritted teeth. "The kids must have told the wife about the pub when they came back with their ice cream, and she'd warned 'em what would happen if they told me about it."

"No more ices," I said.

"It's no laughing matter," he growled, his annoyance, in the shape of clenched fists and scarlet face, beginning to get the better of him. "Wait till I get home," he shouted.

I was beginning to regret having mentioned the pub and made an attempt to calm him down.

"The worst bloody holiday I have ever had, and she knew exactly where I could have enjoyed at least a couple of pints," he shouted

Eleven o'clock came and he stormed out of the station on his way home. If I could have obtained Tom's home telephone number, I would have called Mrs. O'Donnell in an effort to prepare her for the pending domestic dispute. On the other hand, my own rule of never interfering between husband and wife would have prevented my doing so. I have no idea what may have gone on at the O'Donnell household that night, but whatever it was, it didn't prevent the family returning to the resort the following year. Needless to say, I resisted the urge to enquire whether he had enjoyed it or not.

There were, from time to time, welcome breaks from the routine, like training courses. I attended several such breaks, most of which I found enjoyable and instructive. For some reason, motor cars and driving them, has never appealed to me, though many of my colleagues strove to get in to the Transport Section, and once in strove even harder to remain there. The slightest threat that they would be kicked out and back on the beat was a source of terror to them.

I had to attend the driving course in order to become a qualified police driver, but my heart wasn't in it, though I did pass, and was glad to be back on the beat at the end of it. It was, however, a valuable period of instruction, which has served me well all my driving life. That could not be said of another course of three weeks duration, which I was sent on in nineteen sixty four.

Some brilliant mind in Whitehall decided that the Soviet Union was about to direct a bombardment of nuclear weapons upon the United Kingdom, and the police must be trained to deal with the resulting consequences. This was in spite of the fact that there were notices all over Manchester to the effect that the city was a nuclear free zone!

The course was conducted at Easing Wold, a small town in

85

Yorkshire, and the instructors were civilian members of the Home Office staff On the appointed day the police officers selected to take the course were allocated their quarters and introduced to the instructors. Great influence was put upon the seriousness of the training programme, supported by what appeared to be a large village built solely for the purpose of conducting this and future courses.

The Chief Instructor, a diminutive, obnoxious, former naval commander, who chain smoked, found frustration in his dealings with policemen, especially as all thirty of us, being sceptical of the value of the course, were unable to find a remote interest in it.

On the first day, the commander took an instant dislike in me when I asked him a number of questions following his introductory lecture. He had outlined the government's plan whereby in the aftermath of a nuclear attack, the general population where to be prevented from leaving a zone which had borne the brunt of radio activity in order to seek refuge in a less contaminated area.

"How on earth can a handful of coppers stop a couple of million panicking people from fleeing Manchester for the Lake District, or anywhere else?" I innocently asked.

The face of the lecturer turned blood red and then purple as he glared at me. His hands shook violently as he struggled to open a fresh pack of cigarettes.

"That procedure will be revealed to you during the next three weeks," he mumbled.

When a sergeant from the Liverpool force said they didn't want anyone from Manchester to seek shelter there, an argument ensued which had little to do with the subject under discussion. The furious instructor struggled to bring all present to order, and after some success, continued.

"You will be taking place in certain tactical exercises with the view to returning to your force and there training others."

During lunch that first day, it was more or less agreed among the reluctant students that at least it would be three weeks away from shift work, and upon the discovery that the site had a bar, come social room, there prevailed a sense of going along with the pantomime.

The next few days were spent with charts and maps, which outlined the various suggestions as to where the enemy would direct their missiles.

"There will be a four minute warning given by the War Office," explained one of the other instructors.

A few of us had the audacity to enquire as to how this cordon of police officers could be gathered, briefed, and put in to position within the allotted four minutes. The instructor's mouth fell open and silent, to be saved by the bell which called us all to the canteen for lunch. Such was the pattern of the war duties course, but I for one could not drum up the slightest interest.

Most of the policemen there had vivid memories of the Second World War, and how a city could be affected by bombing to the extent that fires alone could develop so rapidly as to be too much for the emergency services to control, let alone the high explosives which were delivered at the same time.

Towards the end of the course it was explained that we would all be armed and that in the event of any civil disobedience with regard to an order to remain in a zone directly contaminated by nuclear fall out, the police would be authorised to fire on those defying the instruction.

Now I didn't mind shooting at the King's enemies, but I drew the line at killing my own countrymen merely because they wished for their kin-folk to get as far away from the fatal dust as possible, and I said so.

At the completion of the course, I was second from the bottom of the class. A sergeant from another force was bottom, but that may have had something to do with him being required to attend court four or five times during the period.

When I returned to my division there was no mention of the course, and though a war duties department was set up, I was not directed to become a member of the training staff.

Chapter Nine

Police officers and the animal kingdom never seem to have got on well together, with certain exceptions. Members of the dog section and the mounted branch, by necessity, have managed to cultivate a relationship between man and beast.

When the dog section was in its infancy I learned an important lesson with regard to the operation of the animals. Together with half a dozen other beat men, I was searching a large area of railway property in an effort to apprehend a group of thieves who had been spotted there breaking in to an office block.

Suddenly the gang broke cover and began to run, followed by ourselves. Two police dog handlers released their gigantic German shepherds, both of which reached us in record time. I naively believed that as they were highly trained animals they would overtake us and bring the crooks down enabling us to affect their arrest at a more leisurely pace. That evening I learnt that when dogs have been trained to detain anybody who is sprinting, it means 'anybody', and that is what these two did. My uniform trousers were ripped from heel to thigh, and it was only when I lay on the ground that the beasts sat down to wait their further instructions from the handlers.

The other officers, who had been similarly running, shared the same fate as myself whilst the thieves succeeded in vanishing in to the warren of houses beyond the goods yard.

One dog handler trained his charge to howl like a wolf whenever he gave it a secret command which related to a certain despised chief superintendent. Should that particular senior officer be anywhere near the dog, the spine chilling wail would be produced for no understandable reason, at least as far as the chief superintendent was aware.

I could never have been described as an animal lover, though I took exception to any cruelty towards them, and whenever I came across a public telephone full of cats I always set the creatures free. It was the practice of some officers, when bored on the night shift, to collect as many felines as they could, and deposit them in those telephone booths!

From time to time, animal movement orders would appear at the stations and it would be the duty of the police to attend the address mentioned for the purpose of inspecting the animals referred to in the order. The purpose of such inspections was to verify whether the animals had suffered during their journey or not.

On the first occasion that I was given a form to complete I went to a busy butcher's shop on my beat. The owner was one of the few remaining butchers who killed his animals on the premises, having purchased them on the hoof.

I explained the purpose of my visit and he said, "You're just in time constable, this lady has just bought the last leg of lamb from that consignment!"

That movement order, like many more, had been lying around on someone's desk instead of being forwarded immediately to the division concerned.

Gypsies, or travellers, as they are referred to nowadays, moved around the country in a more leisurely fashion in the fifties, by way of horse drawn vehicles. Sometimes these delightful people would arrive in the night and park up their caravans on spare ground, usually a patch of land established by Adolph Hitler's Luftwaffe, some five or six years earlier.

For some reason, residents of the area in close proximity to the caravans were not disposed to their temporary neighbours, and by the morning the local station would be inundated with complaints about them.

Amongst the varied mass of allegations was the complaint that horses were allowed to roam free in the district, and there were occasions when such allegations were apparent, though it would be more likely the animals had broken free of their tethers, after all, it is unlikely that their owners would have deliberately allowed them to roam the streets, as it was the duty of the police to impound them and the owner could only reclaim them after paying a sum of money.

The subject arose when I was chatting to my colleague, P.C. Ken Hamlet. "I was on nights and standing at the corner of Queens Road," he recalled. "About two in the morning I heard the clattering of many hooves coming towards me, and through the mist appeared about ten horses, the front one ridden by one of the P.C.s from the next section. He waved at me as he turned his mount into Queens Road, followed obediently by the rest. I learnt later that he had found them on the main road, and being a former farm lad, he had mounted the leader, knowing the rest would follow."

All the group were impounded and retrieved by their owners the following morning.

For a time I worked on an area which encompassed a large zoological garden, and it was strange when on night duty to hear the cries and roars of the many beasts more likely to be heard in the jungles of Africa.

Sometimes the imprisoned creatures effected an escape and were soon recaptured, and it would not be unusual to find some exotic bird flitting around the nearby shopping thoroughfare. Constable Clive Senior put away his uniform in his locker at the sub-station which was opposite to the main entrance of the zoo, then went home to enjoy a well earned day off. When he returned to work, he was informed by the station officer that strange scratching sounds had been heard coming from the interior of his locker.

"It's obvious that a mouse has got in there," said the station officer.

P.C. Senior took his key from his pocket and opened the door of his locker. He reeled backwards, a monkey clawing and attempting to bite him had quit the prison like a bullet from a gun. With deafening screams the beast clung to his hair and it was only the intervention of two other officers in the room which prevented some serious injury to him.

They managed to return the monkey to the locker and close the door, whilst another officer dashed across to the zoo for help. He came back with a young girl who declared that she was an apprentice keeper. Someone opened the locker and everyone withdrew to the opposite end of the room. The girl reached in and drew out the monkey, which quietly snuggled up to her chest, there to be carried back to the relatively peaceful surroundings of the monkey house.

Police officers who belonged to the road traffic patrol division may well believe that they were most unlikely to become directly involved with the animal kingdom, and that if they ever did, would be safe within the protective body work of the vehicle in their charge. Whilst, for instance, dogs may bark and snap at the heels of a beat officer, who, in the hours of daylight is unable to persuade the four legged tormentor to desist, the officer hurtling along the road in his highly charged patrol car will successfully outpace the most determined of canines.

Police constable Daniel Ewington drove the brand new car around the area he was allocated, throughout the afternoon and evening of a pleasant spring day and as the hour his shift was to finish drew close, he decided to take a change of scenery. The patrol he was on was up and down dreary streets where nothing was happening and he decided to have a little run out into a more rural setting.

He turned the car away from the Manchester force area and in to the direction of the jurisdiction of the Lancashire Constabulary. It was his intention to drive at a leisurely pace for a few miles through country lanes which led, ultimately, back to the territory of his own force.

When he was some four miles into forbidden meadow land and slowing to some three miles an hour to avoid pot holes outside a farm, a giant bull appeared at the open gate of the premises. It lowered its head and with what seemed to be a nought to sixty miles an hour in three seconds start, the raging beast charged at the police car. Daniel's hurried attempt to get the vehicle out of the way, failed to avoid one of the bull's horns piercing the driver's door, emerging on the interior and almost pinning him to the seat. The owner of the bull came running and with a great deal of effort, managed to extract the animal from the car and drive it back in to the safety of the farm.

The officer, being obliged to report the incident to both his own superiors and the Lancashire Constabulary, did just that and awaited the attendance of both representatives. Ultimately, the matter was treated as a road accident, and Daniel's explanation to the effect that he had been following a suspected stolen car, which necessitated him leaving his own area, was reluctantly accepted.

The farmer was prosecuted for keeping a none castrated bull without the appropriate licence, and Daniel avoided the awful punishment, that of being returned to working a beat on foot.

New in the rank of sergeant, I felt my way around cautiously, first getting to know the geography of my new division, then the quality of the constables I commanded. Some of those officers were willing to inform the sergeant as to the reliability, or otherwise, of their colleagues, though I preferred to assess them for myself. I walked along the section, on the morning shift, with one of the constables who appeared to me to be suffering from a dreaded ailment I had seen amongst people when serving king and country in Africa.

Apparently, if you are unfortunate enough to be bitten by the tsetse fly, the result is a condition known as sleeping sickness which stays with you for the rest of your life. The lad, between loud expressive yawns, informed me that he and his wife were the occupants of one of the houses provided in those days by the Police Authority. My assessment of the officer, was that he was quite definitely in the wrong job. During the eighteen months he had patrolled in an area of high crime and public disorderliness, he had failed to arrest anyone. He had, however, managed to achieve a reputation for being late for duty when on the morning shift.

I informed him that I would require him to vastly improve, at which he announced that he had submitted his resignation a week earlier. I tried not to register my delight at the news, and enquired as to what new form of employment he was to follow.

"Selling encyclopaedias, sergeant," he announced.

Whit Week walks under police supervision

It was common knowledge that the remuneration in that form of employment was pitifully low, and could only be brought to a reasonable figure by the volume of sales achieved. A set of the books, in the nineteen sixties, cost £1,000, at a time when a very good salary was around £2,000 a year, and I pointed that out to the officer.

"Do you know anything about salesmanship?" I asked.

"No," replied the sleepy constable, "but I went out with the senior sales manager last Wednesday and he showed me how to go about it."

His reply to my question about the number of volumes sold that day was in the negative, the super sales manager having told him that occasionally he could draw a blank. I thought it best, in the interests of the force, not to discourage him, and changed the subject.

"Where will you be going to live?" I asked.

"As I told you sergeant, I live on Mount Road."

I pointed out that he was in a police house, and that in a matter of two weeks he would be required to get out. He came to a sudden halt, and for a moment appeared to have become alert.

"I'd never thought of that," he muttered.

Against my better judgement I directed him to go at once to the divisional H.Q. and withdraw his resignation. Accommodation in those days was very difficult to come by, and many policemen had only joined in order to obtain a house for themselves and their families. The aspiring salesman stayed on in the force for some three months, then successfully applied for a position at a pie, sausage and ice cream manufacturers factory, a few miles up the road.

The hospitality of one police force for another was always an important feature, especially in the case of C.I.D. men. For detectives to visit another police area and not be treated to a memorable night out would be considered a disgrace and unforgivable.

The Lord Abercrombie Inn, near to the entrance of the Bootle Street police station, was where all officers who worked on that division relaxed after duty. It was also the favourite lodgings of visiting officers from other police forces on escort duty or other matters, necessitating an overnight stay. On such occasions, it was usual for detectives on split duties to be instructed to liaise with those visitors.

One evening two 'A' Division officers met up with two detective constables from the Metropolitan Police, at the Abercrombie Affability abounded as further colleagues joined them, and as the evening progressed it was decided to call at the police club, only to discover that it was closed on Mondays. That resulted in a pub crawl in the locality, with excesses developing in every bar visited, and as is always the case a sense of time was the first casualty of the binge.

The group, now some ten or eleven in number, decided to patronise one of the new Asian restaurants which were springing up in the district like wildfire, and there they ordered the hottest dishes available. On the recommendation of the two officers from London, who had been familiar with the fare for some time, they also ordered copious amounts of cold lager to ease their burning mouths.

On leaving the restaurant one of the local detectives said that if they hurried, they might just be in time for a drink at his favourite local, before last orders. He led the party along a couple of dark entries until they arrived at the side door of the Grey Horse. The pathfinder indicated that they should all be a little quieter by holding a finger to his lips, the gave three knocks on the glass panel of the door. One of the others tried the door handle, at which the door opened.

Everybody followed the local man into the bar, where they were taken somewhat aback to find the pub quite full, with the customers making no effort whatsoever to be quiet, and the landlord merrily serving away, with apparent complete disregard for the licensing laws.

"You're taking a bit of a liberty serving with the doors open and everything, aren't you Fred?" said the local officer.

The licensee, pointing to the clock, said, " It's only ten to ten Arthur, eleven is last orders."

The group stayed in the Grey Horse until it was really last orders and then moved back to the city centre, where the Londoners were introduced to various night clubs.

"I'll never know how we didn't all become alcoholics!" remarked one of the old detectives, when I met him some thirty five years later.

There were a small number of our colleagues in fact who did, though hundreds did not, and it is my opinion that when drinking on duty there was a corner of the brain which remained sober

94

and ready to deal with anything requiring a clear head, and that would explain why it was hardly ever noticed by members of the public, law abiding, or otherwise.

Two detectives who rarely if ever imbibed were Superintendent Donald Gibson and Constable Bernard Postles, who together detected a murder, the suspicion of which, the search and discovery of the victim's body, the detection of the perpetrator, his arrest and the charging of him, took a mere one hour and fifteen minutes, a feat believed to be a record to this day.

In 1978, Detective Superintendent Donald Gibson was the officer commanding the C.I.D. at the new police headquarters in east Manchester. He lived several miles from that location, and due to circumstances, was entitled to be transported to and from the office by police vehicle. As such, the detective constable who had been on duty during the night was obliged to take the C.I.D. car and pick him up from his home each morning at a quarter to seven.

On the morning of the occurrence he was collected by Detective Constable Postles and the journey began. As they reached the division there was a message over the radio to the effect that a man had been seen carrying an apparently unconscious man over his shoulder. The officers, who were only a few hundred yards from the location of the sighting, informed the Information Room that they were attending. There was nobody about as they turned into a disused business yard, where they left the vehicle and commenced to search.

"It began to look like a false report," said Don. "We decided to leave when I noticed a group of waste bins against a wall. As a last resort Bernard and I inspected the bins and discovered a dead man, aged about fifty. He had been deposited head first into the bin and I noticed that his right leg had been almost broken in half, presumably to afford a better fit".

The pair walked to a row of terraced cottages, which lay close to the entrance of the yard, and on seeing the front door of one of them was ajar, they stepped inside.

"There was a passage which led in to the kitchen, and in there we found a man aged about thirty five. He looked up at us from an old armchair and fixed me with a stare. I knew instinctively that we had found the murderer, and before we could begin to question him, he asked us if we had found his father.

"He went on to say that there had been bad feelings between them for many years, and alleged that his father had abused him from childhood. He told how that morning they had yet another row, during which he struck his parent with an axe and carried his body out to the bins."

Superintendent Gibson and his colleague arrested the young man, and after instructing a couple of uniformed officers who had arrived at the scene, with regard to the removal of the body, they conveyed their prisoner to the police station, where he was charged with murder.

Under two hours had passed since the original radio message, and postponing the necessary paper work in order to attend to other pressing matters caused Donald to omit the important duty of telling his senior officers at headquarters about the murder.

"They were receiving requests for information from the press, and having to admit they knew nothing about a murder," said the superintendent.

Detective Constable Bernard Postles had impressed his superintendent that day as he ably assisted in the affair. He went on become a Detective Chief Superintendent and famously conducted the case against Doctor Harold Shipman, Britain's most prolific killer who was found guilty of murdering elderly people whilst they were his patients.

When you have a police force area which is totally covered by men on foot, day and night, bank holidays and holy days included, there is little which goes unnoticed. During my early days as a cop it was unusual to be allocated a beat with less than around eight thousand souls residing within its borders, and there was one such beat with something like twenty thousand.

These areas were chiefly made up of small terraced houses, then getting on for a hundred years old, and originally erected to accommodate the high numbers of people engaged in the heavy industry of the time. Beer houses abounded, the proprietors of which took a high proportion of the locals' hard earned wages. The main roads, which ran through these districts, were the locations of hundreds of shops, which provided all needs, often on a tick or slate arrangement.

Similarly, clothes were purchased on the basis of wear now pay later. Pawn shops, strategically sited, helped out in times of financial difficulty, when people handed the old man's suit, or anything else for that matter, over the counter to obtain a loan. The item could be redeemed later by paying the required amount, and if the statutory period of pawning ran out the pawnbroker could sell it on.

One of the many pawnbrokers was known as Piggy Riley, he having taken in to pawn a full grown pig! These particular businessmen, found it wise to co-operate with the police, and many a customer attempting to unload stolen property found themselves arrested.

There was a daily publication, called Pawnbroker Bill, which listed and described stolen items, and the lists were delivered through the letter boxes of every pawn shop by the officer on the beat during the early hours of each day. That practice, in addition to bringing to the notice of the broker the goods in question, put him in an awkward position should he be caught accepting property which had been shown on the list, and attempting to plead that he was unaware that it was stolen.

It was a regular occurrence for the beat man to find, in the night, that the occupants of houses had repaired to their beds having failed to secure the front door. Very often that oversight could be attributed to forgetfulness due to drink. Police Constable Ken Hamlet, whilst patrolling one night, found such an omission in a Collyhurst street.

"It was about one in the morning and the door was wide open, the key was in the lock and I stepped in to the tiny front room. The place was in darkness and I made use of my torch as I examined the downstairs area.

"The lighting of the houses round there was provided by gas, so it wasn't a case of flicking the light switch as we would today. I made my way up the creaking stairs, where I heard someone loudly groaning, and I entered a bedroom. I shone my torch on to a bed in and was startled to see a man and woman in the throes of conjugal bliss!

"The woman turned her face towards me, and you could be forgiven for thinking that it was a regular occurrence for a large policeman to shine his torch on to her in her own home whenever she and her spouse made love. She seemed to ignore my presence completely, her husband too, although it has to be said his face was buried in to a pillow." related the officer.

He withdrew from the scene and left the premises, leaving the key on a sideboard and quietly closing the front door behind him!

Chapter Ten

Criticism of the police has gone on since 1829 when the first ever constabulary was born, and I suppose it will continue until some time in the future when it becomes replaced by some other form of preserving law and order.

During the nineteen fifties, there was an eminent City Councillor who took it upon himself to mastermind a vicious campaign against the force on the basis, as he put it, that the Chief Constable had chosen, for some reason, to ignore the presence of hundreds of prostitutes who gathered nightly on the streets of the city centre offering to perform lewd practises for cash.

Championing the campaign was one of the two evening papers, popular at the time. To an extent, the councillor was right; there were a great many of these women to be found strutting about in the areas he mentioned, but the law at the time did not make such behaviour a criminal act.

Some effort was always made to remedy the situation and large numbers of the girls were regularly arrested and charged with the offence of 'obstructing the footpath'. Many of their customers, having chosen one of the women on display, would then hail a taxi in which to be transported to some dingy house or apartment just outside the city, wherein the transaction would be completed to the satisfaction of at least, the client.

Around one thirty on a chilly December morning, I was patrolling my beat when a young probationary constable crossed the road from his beat to speak to me.

"There's a posh car parked at the bottom of Adelide Street," he informed me.

What would not appear to be unusual today was odd in those days. The street mentioned was in an extremely rough district, full of low life, at number eleven there was a brothel, and on inspection I found the front door to be unlocked. I knew that prostitutes entertained their customers on a rather filthy mattress in the front room and I could hear voices from there.

With the other officer I walked in. A single low wattage light bulb barely illuminated the filthy stinking room, but it was sufficient for us to see a woman who was lying on the mattress, half dressed, and a middle aged man kneeling at the edge, he too being partly dressed. Another middle aged man, his trousers about his ankles, was sitting in a threadbare armchair under the window. After everyone had complied with my request to adjust their clothing, there were vociferous protests from the tubby chap who had been sitting with his pants down.

At that stage my colleague whispered to me that he had recognised, from a photograph in the campaigning newspaper, that the man doing all the complaining was in fact the troublesome councillor. I turned to him and told him that I knew he was that person and that in view of his bitter campaign wherein he denounced the police for permitting the very trade he had been encouraging, I would be making a report to my superiors.

I obtained the particulars of the other man, and with a wink towards the prostitute, whom I knew to be 'Welsh Winnie' I and the other constable left to return to our beats. The subsequent report submitted by myself caused the Chief Superintendent to send for me. He went over the events for about an hour, then, with a broad grin, told me not to discuss the matter with anyone. The newspaper articles ceased immediately and little was heard of the people's champion afterwards.

The probationary constable who had first drawn my attention to the events at the Adelide Street brothel, had an unfortunate affliction in the form of a nervous habit which caused him to nod his head furiously from time to time, earning him the unavoidable nickname of 'Noddy'. Some years following our adventure at the brothel, I was on office duties at a police station covering the north of the division when 'Noddy' turned up for a spell of traffic duty at the busy junction just outside the station.

He was, as all of us were, highly trained in the regulation of traffic by hand signals. He donned the appropriate white traffic sleeves and went out to signal the rush hour drivers safely over the crossroads. A few minutes later an unearthly bang and screeching of brakes was heard. and a couple of officers who were taking their breakfasts dashed outside to investigate. One of them came back in with two injured men and I called an ambulance.

A glance from the door revealed a scene of chaos, with traffic piled up everywhere. In the middle of the junction were two cars and a van, which were obvious write offs, whilst 'Noddy' and other officers were endeavouring to sort it all out. I asked those awaiting medical attention what had happened and one of the drivers explained.

"I was driving towards the junction when the constable in the centre of the road put up his hand in a clear signal for me to stop, which of course I did. He then began to signal the other traffic over the junction. Then, he looked straight at me and nodded his head three or four times. I thought he was telling me to come on, which I did, and drove straight into a bloody van."

The other individual involved in the affair of the erring councillor, 'Welsh Winnie', became less and less attractive as the years passed, and as such, her earning power deteriorated. She took the path of all who followed the trade and sought solace, first from gin, then inevitably from mentholated spirits.

Her party piece took the form of seeking out very young policemen in busy thoroughfares and stripping off her clothes. She would then jump on the hapless constable, fasten her rotten teeth on his nose and cling like a lamprey. The harder the victim pushed to free himself, the more painful the grip on the ravaged proboscis, and eventually the officer would be obliged to carry her through the crowds to the station.

Not long before I was promoted to the rank of sergeant, and probably because with thirteen years service as a constable I had become qualified for the odd cushy job, I was instructed to take the place of an older colleague at a former police radio station sited in the centre of the largest public park in the United Kingdom.

The building, constructed of wood, lay alone in an area of meadows to which the public had no access. It was some mile and a half from the main gates, which at night were locked, and the only person in the vast grounds was the policeman at the old radio building. Whilst the station had been long replaced by the information room at Police Headquarters six miles away in the city centre, there remained a great deal of the original equipment on the premises.

The requirement was for a constable to be there on each of the three shifts, 6 am to 2 p.m.; 2 p.m to 10 p.m.; and ten p.m. to 6 a.m., in the role of watchman. The three officers were found by my own division and had been carrying out the duty on a permanent basis for some eight or nine years. One of the men had gone sick and I had been chosen to take over his duties until such time as he recovered.

It had been the first night of his tour on the ten p.m. to six a.m. shift, and as I lived close to the park I set off on foot in time to reach the station by ten. The walk from the main gate through an inky blackness of winding paths and the shuffling branches of tall trees was an eerie journey, and I was glad when after negotiating a couple of hundred yards of steep incline, I reached the bright lights of the station.

The officer on the afternoon shift, Danny Ewington, was standing at the door and I felt glad that I had arrived ten minutes early so that he could get away.

"Where have you been?" he shouted as I approached. "We have an arrangement up here that the night man gets here at nine so the afternoon man is able to get away in time for a couple of pints. Also, the night man stays here until nine so that the morning man can have a lie in."

He quickly conducted a tour of the building, then leaping onto his cycle, called over his shoulder, "Don't let the dial get to above forty five."

As he rode in to the darkness I called out, "What dial?" but he was by then pedalling at speed towards the main gates.

I can not recall ever before or after the feeling of utter isolation which I experienced that night. A search of the premises revealed a small kitchen with a battered electric kettle and a few cracked cups. In a cupboard there was a tin box containing tea, and that was it. I had, in the normal course of events, brought a bag of sandwiches.

There was a long corridor off which were several rooms, some locked, others not. In a large room at the head of the building a wall completely occupied by a complicated cabinet of clocks and dials producing a symphony of whirring and clicks, with an occasional flashing of small lights. In the middle of the confusion was a sort of clock face upon which there was a needle darting between the numbers , zero and forty five. I found a stool and seating myself in front of the console, prepared to watch the needle of the gauge throughout the night.

I was acutely aware that my situation was similar to that of a goldfish in a bowl, as there were no curtains or blinds, the lights illuminating the interior making me clearly visible to anyone outside, whilst I was incapable of seeing more than an inch into the darkness. After about two hours the gauge and its constant leaping needle became almost hypnotic, and from time to time I dozed.

At around midnight I was alerted by noises outside the building and the sound of something banging a side wall. There were further indications of movement and I decided to investigate. I knew a certain inspector was on nights who was the type of person who took great pleasure in causing the maximum distress to the officers under his command, and I suspected it was he who was creeping around outside in an effort to catch me out and put me on a disciplinary charge. After some difficulty, I found the light switches, and after plunging the place in darkness, I opened the door and leapt outside. I was immediately confronted by a small herd of Highland Cattle, which I later discovered had been introduced to the park only a few weeks earlier.

They stared for a second or two, then turning their backs on me, strolled nonchalantly away. Back in the building I re-lit the station, and seeing that the needle of the gauge was still hovering beneath the figure forty five, I repaired to the kitchen where I made a cup of tea and consumed my sandwiches. From then until nine in the morning when the officer on the next shift turned up, I slipped between staring at the gauge and cat napping.

The constable, looking refreshed from his late rising, enquired if I had settled in.

"Looks like you'll be with us for a while, old Charlie's real bad with his chest," he announced.

I told him that I didn't fancy the job and explained that watching that bloody clock all night wasn't for me.

"You mean you ain't had a kip?" he asked, and beckoning me to follow him down the corridor, he opened one of doors to reveal a single bed with appropriate bedding.

"That's where we spend a fortnight on the night shift. That's why we come on early and go off late. You can then spend all day at home like somebody normal."

I asked about the dial and he informed me that it had never gone over and that should it ever do so, the appropriate action would automatically be taken at the headquarters station. As I staggered down the paths towards the main gates and home, I began to very much look forward to what turned out to be a wonderful summer on duty at the radio station.

Whether it be for the good, or not, the practice of the officers on the beat doling out summary justice to violent individuals appears to be now a thing of the past. There were many officers who were a great deal tougher than any of the local thugs, and often on a Saturday night when the crowds left their favourite drinking parlours to wend their way home, they would be treated to the spectacle of one of the local champions receiving chastisement from a heavy weight wearing a helmet.

The champ would make some sort of a valiant stand for a moment or two, then seek the usual sanctuary of the defeated by feigning unconsciousness. Quite often the termination of the bout would bring applause from the crowd, particularly if the beaten individual had been spoiling what should have been a convivial evening's drinking.

One of the constables, infamous for striking fear into the unlawful side of the population was Harry Dick, a large man, who appeared to hate everyone, including his colleagues, and, some said, himself.

My first experience of the man was on a bright summer evening when we strolled together along Bury New Road close to the prison at Strangeways. Groups of men stood outside several of the pubs, the licensees having stopped serving for the night, and as we drew near, each gathering melted away, presumably to their nearby homes. At the end of the road we turned to retrace our steps and I was astounded to see that apart from the odd person or two walking, presumably from the city centre, the road was deserted.

Harry retired in the late fifties and took a pub in a small town outside Manchester. The premises had the reputation of being a 'fighting house' and uncontrollable. There had been many previous managers, none of whom had remained for more than a few months, and the brewery, having interviewed Harry, came to the conclusion that they had at long last discovered the right man for the post, as indeed they had.

About four months later I saw him in Manchester and asked him how the pub was going.

"Finished there," he snarled.

Mrs. Dick, who was with him, wearily explained that so rough a clientele, refusing to change their drunken manner, had one by one been given the hiding of their lives by her dear husband!

"At one time the customers had a ward of their own at the local hospital," she joked. "In the end they'd had enough and went off to try and find a boozer that they could upset without getting knocked about for their trouble."

The outcome of the situation was that the place became like a mausoleum. It is a well known fact in the public house business that if you miraculously change a fighting house into a normal haven of conviviality, the public are hesitant to immediately come along and try it, result, no trade for a very long time. In other words: 'You can't polish a turd!'

Chatting with one of my constables, he got on to the subject of girls as he, being single and fancy free, was in a position to put himself about. The boy had only been in the job for about six months but was able to inform me of a great number of conquests, which I didn't disbelieve, as the section we were working was well known for the deterioration of morals, heralded by the early nineteen sixties.

I attempted to give the officer a gentle hint as to where his gallivanting could end up.

"I knew a man once," I said, as we strolled by a local dance hall, the source of his supply of female company. " He's dead now, poor feller, and he left three widows mourning their unrepairable loss, he told me that with all his experience women were as much of a riddle to him, as when he first married forty years before.

As only to be expected the young officer wasn't interested in any advice from the voice of experience, nor, I daresay, was I at his age. It was on the next tour of afternoons that the young Lothario was on my section, and meeting him on his beat, we got round, once again to the subject of his hobby.

"Met a darling a fortnight ago sarge," he announced as he pushed out his chest. "Lives up here."

He pointed to one of the streets off the main road. The constable continued with an account of his visit to the girl's house, the previous Saturday.

"Her mother made a big fuss of me and after tea her dad showed me round the house. In the kitchen he pointed out the fittings he had installed, and the terrific job he had made of the brand new bathroom. Then he proudly boasted that everything was knocked off from his place of employment, that big suppliers near the railway station."

I asked the officer whether the girl knew him to be a police officer and he replied that, in keeping with his own policy, he never told any girls what he did for a living. I took a mental note of the

104

address, and the next day I called round to see the occupier. Inside the premises I said that I had called to see the magnificent job he had done in the kitchen and bathroom. I toured the house with him and congratulated him on his expertise, then I enquired whether it was true that he had stolen the materials from his employer. He made an instant confession and I took him off to the station to be charged.

He asked me who had shopped him, and in the same breath suggested to me that it must have been Harold or Mick at work. I made no comment and assumed that he had shown so many neighbours and friends his work that he had not thought of my real informant. When I discovered that the officer had moved on to another section and another girl friend, I could not dismiss the hope that her daddy might be a receiver of stolen property.

Among the myriad of extraneous duties a constable. was required to perform was that of dropping whatever he might be doing in order to promptly attend one or other of the road junctions through which one of Her Majesty's Judges may be passing. When the Assize or Quarter session courts were sitting, the judges were in what was loosely termed, their 'lodgings' in the Salford City area, and in their trips between there and the location of the Minshull Street Court, the officers on beats through which they were transported bore the responsibility of their safe and unhindered progress.

Their transportation took place in the form of Rolls-Royce motor cars belonging to the City Council, driven by a police officer in uniform and accompanied by an armed detective. The main cavalcade swept through our area, passing Strangeways Prison and on in to the city at around nine each morning.

The return journeys were the most inconvenient as they involved some judges leaving the courts earlier than their colleagues, particularly in the afternoon or early evening. Not least of the problems, were the lunchtime movements, for although they left for the lodgings more or less around twelve and returned for a two o'clock resumption, the numbers of officers required to facilitate a smooth passage were depleted by themselves fitting in their periods of refreshment; added to the problems were the sudden decisions of some judges to return to the court earlier or later than the others.

All this, of course, was before the invention of personal radios through which the constables involved might be informed of sudden changes of plan. No excuse for any holding up of their smooth passage would be tolerated by these learned gentlemen, who no doubt believed that the police officers concerned were on duty exclusively to wave them through, and that other officers were taking care of the rest of the divisions in the same way perhaps that Her Majesty may be forgiven for thinking that the length and breadth of her realm smells of fresh paint.

When the new Crown Courts were opened in the early sixties, someone hit upon the excellent idea of having a private dining room for the judges on the premises thereby effectively cutting out, once and for all, the necessity for their lordships to attend their lodgings at lunchtime.

On the opening day the judges were informed of the arrangement, and at noon trooped in to the appointed area. What they had not been made aware of was the fact that when tenders were invited to catering firms for one of them to provide the necessary facilities throughout the building, public tea rooms and the judges dining room, the contract was afforded to one of the City Councillors, who owned such a catering business.

That business was a thriving concern and the cafes it ran in the city were patronised by thousands of shoppers and office employees every day. On the day of the opening of the court, all their lordships were conducted in to their private canteen at lunchtime and took their seats at the plain but serviceable plastic tables. The Lord Chief Justice was present, to mark the importance of the occasion, and it was he who asked the catering manager for the wine list.

"No wine 'ere mate," he announced to the somewhat taken aback dignitary. "Tea, coffee, milk shakes or cordials."

Others were reading the menu cards to be found at each of the tables. Egg on toast, beans on toast and cheese on toast took pride of place, followed down the list by other mouth watering delicacies like meat and potato pie or pastie with chips. Nowhere could be found pheasant suffle, coeurs de palmers, grilles diable or savarin et a babas, some favourites of those present.

They rose to a man and followed the lord chief justice, who had suggested they repair to the lodgings for lunch. A panic ensued, as the drivers, believing they would not be required until the afternoon, were no longer standing by in the yard, and the divisions through which the Rolls Royces would now be racing had instructed the officers that there would be no lunchtime requirement.

Somehow the starving justices reached their destination, dined in the manner to which they were accustomed, and got back to court in one piece. The room set aside for their lordships, was closed down and never used again for the purpose for which it had been designated, but on the numerous occasions when I dined in the less important eating places within the court buildings, I was perfectly happy with what was on offer.

On one of the last occasions I took refreshment there, I met Detective Sergeant Benny Paris, with whom I had served with for several years when we were constables.

The usual greeting, " What are you here with?" passed between us.

"Bloke stealing electric," I said.

"Lad pinching money with his girlfriend," was his reply.

The formalities dispensed with, other topics were discussed until we parted for the separate courts involved.   Later in the day I ran across another old colleague.

"Just been in number one court," he said, and went on to relate a case he had been watching. He said that Benny Paris was in the mire and I asked him to elaborate.

"Well he'd charged a youth with stealing a pound note from one of the department stores. Apparently the lad's bird is a cashier on one of the tills and he was seen to approach the girl where she slipped him a quid from the till. The store detective grabbed him, took the pound note off him, checked the till, which was a pound short and rang the police. Benny was sent over and he arrested and charged the thieves. It seems he placed the pound note into the property room as an exhibit in the case where it was meant to remain until the trial and entered up properly of course in the normal way.

Both miscreants had pleaded not guilty and it was some seven months before the case came on at the Crown Court. Ben collected the pound note from the station and made his way across the city centre to the imposing house of correction. He purchased a newspaper and a tube of cough sweets at a kiosk on the way, and as he entered the building, he realised that he had paid for the items with the exhibit!

He was not unduly concerned when checking his pocket he discovered another pound note amongst his money. In court, he slipped the bank note onto the table with an appropriate label.

The tribunal was well under way, and the defending barrister, having ripped the store detective apart with a barrage of scathing remarks designed to turn her in to a gibbering wreck called for the detective sergeant to enter the witness box. Ben, like all police officers who made it their business to maintain a vast experience of cross questioning in court, parried the efforts of the legal aid champion to confuse him, until asked about the exhibit.

The pound note was passed to him by the usher, and the barrister asked, "You took possession of that one pound note at the time of arresting the accused persons, did you not?"

"That is true," replied Ben.

"Are you absolutely certain, did you make a note of it, the serial number and so on?" enquired his adversary.

Ben had omitted to record the particulars of the original note, nor had he jotted down that of the one he was at present holding. He admitted that he had not recorded the number.

" Then," boomed the lawyer, grasping the lapels of his gown, in true Dickension fashion. "How can you be so positive that what you are holding there, is in fact a note which you have told us you had taken from the accused at the time of their arrest?"

"Because it has been kept in a locked cupboard and room at the police station" replied the officer.

To his relief he was asked to step down from the witness box, to be replaced by a smartly dressed man, who on taking the oath, introduced himself to be an official of the Mint.

"Can you tell the court anything about this Bank Of England note?" asked the barrister.

The expert studied the exhibit for a few seconds, then in a loud voice, announced that it belonged to a batch which was printed two months earlier.

"If I were to ask you whether it could possibly be in circulation on the date of my clients' arrest, what would you say?"

It flashed through Benny's mind that he should run out of the court, leap in his car and make for the airport, he told me later.

" I would tell you that it would be quite impossible," the witness replied.

The thieves, on the evidence of the man from the mint, were acquitted and Benny had to submit a report on the matter. The next day he was seen by the Detective Chief Superintendent, who listened to his account with a sympathetic ear born of his own little mistakes in the past, and allowed to remain in the department.

Chapter Eleven

I worked hard to stay out of two situations; one, office work, because I preferred to be out where it was all happening, two driving police vehicles, for all sorts of reasons.

Needless to say, I did find myself doing inside duties from time to time, and driving when it couldn't be avoided. To be fair, I did receive a high degree of training in the handling of vehicles under the expert tuition of colleagues in the police driving school. Courses devised in the nineteen thirties at Hendon Police College, the format of which continues unaltered to this day, resulted in those officers successful in passing becoming qualified to drive many of the cars and vans maintained by the force.

Those who excelled on basic courses were selected to attend further, more advanced, training in order that they may be selected to drive anything in general, and the super fast road patrol vehicles in particular.

At each police station, after nineteen sixty seven, there was provided a car for each beat man, a car for the inspector and another for use by the sergeant Being one of the old school, I believed that policemen could get themselves into enough trouble without the help of a motor car, and in consequence, whenever I was the section sergeant, the allocated vehicle rarely turned a wheel.

However, on a particularly wet Sunday morning, I had a number of addresses which I had to visit in respect of witnesses to a fatal accident which had taken place the night before, and I was obliged to use a car. At around two o'clock in the afternoon I was driving along a main road towards the station when a general call came over the radio.

One of the officers on my section had discovered a man breaking in to a pharmacy, and by chance the location was only a couple of hundred yards from my own position. In fact, when I looked across a stretch of derelict land to my left, I could see the constable at the rear of the shop struggling with a large man. I turned on to the land and bumped along what had once been a cobbled street.

Some half way across the area there stood a public house, out-side of which was a group of men, presumably lunchtime cus-tomers about to stagger off home. What remained of the old street was covered in potholes which were filled with water from the per-sistent downpour, and through which the car bounced as I bore down on the scuffling pair. I reached the shop and was soon restraining the offender. After transporting him and the officer to the station, I put the car away and that was that.

The next day, on arrival at the station, I was approached by a newly promoted inspector.

"I am dealing with a serious complaint against you sergeant," he said. "I understand that you deliberately drove a police vehicle through a puddle, and in doing so you caused a large amount of water to rise up and splash a group of men."

At first I thought he was pulling my leg , but his attitude was such that I could see he was serious.

"I have been to the home of one of the complainants and he has shown me his brand new suit which I found to be ringing wet."

I asked the inspector whether the suit was also muddy, for as I pointed out, the spare land and former street, was a mass of mud. The investigator admitted to me that there had been no mud on the garment.

"He's dipped it in the bath when he knew you were coming, sure-ly that must have occurred to you," I said.

From that moment and for the ensuing seven weeks, the matter took on the importance of a major crime. A short time before the incident, a department had been formed, into which numerous high ranking C.I.D. officers had been drafted, and their new role was to be the investigation of complaints against police officers.

They were required in such strength as a result of the new Police Act of 1964, which, to the delight of all criminals, set out the new how to complain about the police procedure. Many of the crooks made good use of the new law as a method of avoiding prosecu-tion.

I was interviewed a couple of times with regard to the incident and at length I was informed that to drive through water and con-sequently splash a pedestrian constituted a criminal offence, as was that of driving a motor vehicle without reasonable considera-tion for other road users. The whole matter was being sent to the Director Of Public Prosecutions, in London, for him to decide on whether I should be tried before a court. Some five months later, my own superintendent sent for me and as I entered his office I saw the familiar D.P.P. yellow bound file on his desk.

The package was some six inches thick, representing many hours of work on behalf of its composers.

"The Home Office have sent this lot back having extensively perused it all, and they have decided that there is insufficient evidence to support a prosecution against you," said the superintendent with one of his famous smirks.

He sported several hairs on the bridge of his nose, and it was only with a supreme effort that I was able to resist a temptation to reach across his desk and tug them out, one by one. Instead, I contented myself with laughing out loud, a reaction which infuriated him.

"You may find all this amusing but I don't," he yelled.

Going through my mind was the fact that whilst the investigation of my heinous crime was taking place, a detective sergeant friend of mine was unable to get any help with an enquiry he was conducting into an attempted murder of a young man who had been taken onto a car park and there battered about his head with some heavy instrument. "There was no one available that week," he told me.

Months after the encounter, I was in the charge office when the obnoxious superintendent was about to go off duty.

"Sergeant," he said. " At half past seven, ring me at home."

There was no further conversation and he left the office. I became involved with a serious accident and it wasn't until eleven that I remembered, by then there was no point in my telephoning him. The next day I explained my reason for neglecting to ring and to my surprise he merely shrugged his shoulders. I discussed the incident with another sergeant, who enlightened me on the subject.

"He does it regularly," he told me. " When you ring him his wife always answers and she then brings him to the phone. He then asks you why you can't contact another senior officer and plays hell for a couple of seconds, after which he puts the phone down."

In reply to my question as to why, my colleague informed me that the superintendent had a woman on the side, and by making his dear wife believe he had to turn out to some occurrence, he would be free for a clandestine meeting, perhaps overnight. I confess to entertaining thoughts of an anonymous letter, quickly abandoned when I remembered it was the wife who would be more upset than he.

Females in the police were not accepted as being on a par with male officers until the late nineteen seventies, when at long last they were granted equal pay. They first appeared around nineteen thirteen, and were auxiliaries until shortly after the Second World War, when the Home Office managed to persuade chief constables to recruit more ladies.

Gradually, and reluctantly, a limited few were accepted into the various police forces, under certain conditions, firstly, that their stipend would fall short of that meagre pittance of the men, and that they would not be required to emulate the duties of their male colleagues, for example, work on a division as a beat officer, or be sent to perform any duty during the hours of darkness without the express instruction of a senior officer.

These girls operated under the title of Policewoman and received identical training to that of the men, spending their first three months at the district training centre. As in any walk of life, there were complications, not least, those resulting from throwing both sexes together in a residential establishment.

The instructors, all sergeants or inspectors, each taught a class of around twenty in which there were usually two or three women officers. One of the instructors, a long thin individual who reminded us of a popular film character, Frankenstein's Monster, a resemblance I hadn't noticed until one of the lads asked me if someone had pinched the bolt out of his neck, was sent back to his force for forming an improper association with one of the female students in his class, whilst she was dismissed.

I was not alone in trying to understand what a pretty girl of twenty found attractive about the inspector, a married man some twenty two years her senior.

"If I was a woman and he came anywhere near me, I'd dial 999," I said to one of the other policewomen sitting opposite me in the canteen the following day.

"Well it's power that does it," she explained. "Him being of inspector rank and sitting up there at the front of the class must have got her going I suppose."

The policewomen took up their equal duties with the men just before I retired from the service. I have to say that I was not relishing the idea of having any of the women on my section, particularly on nights, as I honestly believed that they should not be directed to walk about on their own on the violent streets of the district.

The seedy dark entries along which the beat man, now beat woman, had to negotiate in order to carry out regular inspections of vulnerable property, were places in which many an officer, having disturbed or captured thieves, had to employ a maximum effort and fighting strength in order to avoid serious injury, let alone successfully detain miscreants.

Of course, there were a number of female officers who were as capable of carrying out those duties equally as well as their male counterparts, as many a tough guy has discovered, but in the case of the majority I felt uneasy.

Reluctant to have the girls on my section, I was nevertheless glad to employ them during the daylight hours when hundreds of telephone calls made to the police, most of which were nothing to do with us, nevertheless needed to be answered.

On a quiet Sunday morning, I was taking my breakfast at the station when I was informed that a man, who resided alone, had not been seen for more than a week and that his daily delivery of milk was piling up on his step. There were two female officers about to go out and I instructed them to attend the address.

"If you can't get in easily, ask a neighbour to push the door in for you," I said, as they were leaving.

About an hour and a half later, the clerk called me to the phone.

"It's a mister Rawton and he's in a bit of a state," he informed me.

"Is that sergeant Wood?" the caller stammered very excitedly. I said that it was and he continued.

"You ought to be thoroughly ashamed about what you have done to my daughter," he said.

I had not done anything to be ashamed of to anybody's daughter for many years, and told him so.

"I understand that you made her go to a house where a man had hung himself. She's in bed now at home and we've sent for the doctor."

I hung up and made one of my infrequent trips in a Panda Car to the scene of the suicide. As I drew up at the address I could see one of the girls I had sent to the address sitting on the doorstep crying. A group of neighbours were attempting to comfort her with cups of tea, one of whom, a young man, informed me that at her

113

request he had kicked open the door and accompanied another policewoman into the kitchen where they found the occupier's body hanging by his neck on a rope tied to the clothes rack.

I went in to the kitchen and cut the unfortunate man down, then discovering that the other female constable had left I was obliged to organise the removal of the deceased and complete the matter myself. On returning to the station some time later I was informed that the missing officer had taken the example of her colleague, having reported sick and gone home.

Shortly after the incident I handed in my uniform to spend the rest of my service in plain clothes and in the C.I.D, and so never came in to contact with either of the constables who found the job so undesirable.

By Christmas I was well entrenched in the role of Crime Prevention Officer, and during the early part of the festive season I received a request from the Regional Security Manager of a large supermarket group for my assistance in a serious problem of shortages at one of their shops on my area. We met by appointment at the store, where he outlined the situation.

"I've spent weeks looking in to a serious shortfall in this place, thousands of pounds involved and I've come up with nothing," he groaned, "so I thought you might be able to throw a new light on it for me."

He closed the door of the office then continued: " I actually

Policing outside Exchange Railway Station.

114

moved one of my own security lads here, undercover of course, and even the manager of the branch doesn't know about that as he just applied for the vacancy in the normal manner. He's been working on the loading bay where everything comes in and he reports nothing lacking in the booking in and out of goods."

I outlined all those areas of dishonesty employed by the staff of retail operations and asked whether he had examined them.

"You know, till staff charging relatives and friends two pounds for twenty pounds worth of goods, this store is in the right area for that one. Is it possible for someone working on the loading bay to be walking away having just counted a delivery in and signed for it? If they do, unscrupulous drivers have a tendency to throw something back on and drive off."

I went on with opportunities often seized by cleaners and many more tricks of the trade.

"No member of staff is allowed to shop in here on their day off even," interrupted the security chief.

It did appear to me that the security chief knew what he was about and seemed to have explored every possible trick. He introduced me to the manager of the store, a thirty year old somewhat dynamic personality, full of enthusiasm and totally fitting the bill as a dedicated company man. He too was at a loss in respect of the shortfall, the situation, as he told me, reflecting on himself and his future with the group.

Before leaving, I took a mental note of the layout of the premises and asked to be furnished with the particulars of everybody employed in those positions of high vulnerability, the cash office, goods in, and the like, in order to ascertain they had people of good character. The security chief invited me to a liquid lunch at the nearby Lord Nelson, and over a pork pie and stout, we went over all the possible areas of shortfall available.

"Firstly," I said, "we've got the thirty one tills."

"Thirty tills," interrupted my companion.

"No, I counted thirty one checkouts and each one manned."

The security manager took out the plan of the premises and counted out the checkout installations.

"Look, it's definitely thirty," he announced. We quickly drank up and hurried back to the supermarket, where we stood back and checked the sites.

"You're right, thirty one," my friend conceded.

We went to see the manager in his office where the security chief

115

asked for an explanation. To my surprise he confessed immediately to having installed the extra checkout himself. The pretty young girl who operated the till and checkout was in fact his girlfriend with whom he secretly resided some twenty miles away from the store.

They had been successful in keeping their relationship a secret for eighteen months, in order to allay suspicion, by his constant admonishing and humiliation of his accomplice in front of the rest of the staff.

All the sales conducted on till thirty one were pocketed by the manager. There were of course no complaints from customers, who had selected their goods and paid for them in the normal manner. The company, fast on its way to growing in to the massive concern it is today, saw fit not to prosecute the couple who had stolen thousands of pounds from them and had merely dismissed them so as to escape publicity, and as far as I am aware, went on to live happily ever after in the firm belief that there really is a Santa Claus.

I told the security manager not to mention me in his report and to take the credit himself, which he apparently did judging by the size of the Christmas hamper he sent me!

The next occasion on which I found my Home Office training in crime prevention to be of benefit to large scale business was in response to a request from the manager of a huge entertainment complex in East Manchester. Among the many facilities to be enjoyed was the twice weekly antics of motor cyclists as they raced around a track showering the fans with cinders, a set of circumstances to which the eager spectators appeared to have little objection.

The freshly appointed manager of the entertainment centre invited me to join him in his office, and later in the several bars under his control. I spotted a few incidents of malpractice amongst his large staff of operatives, and on return to the office enquired about shortages in the takings.

"The worst area is the speedway," he sighed. "The entrance fee is two pounds a person, and I swear that half of 'em must be getting in by avoiding the turnstiles somehow."

He went on to inform me that his predecessor had lost his job through poor receipts, and that he had promised to rectify the situation. I felt that here was a young family man trying to make the

best of himself in a cruel world and that he needed to be introduced to the fact that not everyone was as pious as they would
like us all to believe.

I asked to look at the books relating to the turnstile mystery and
noted that there were eighteen.

"Who mans them?" I asked.

The manager replied that they were all middle aged men, most
of whom had operated the turnstiles every Wednesday and
Saturday for quite a few years. My thoughts drifted back to the
supermarket with the extra till, but it was soon apparent it was
not the problem here.

I asked to be given the names and addresses of the turnstile
chaps, and they were duly produced. A cursory perusal informed
me that some individuals lived as far away as Blackpool,
Blackburn, Liverpool, and in two cases, Leeds. Most of the
remainder were locals in that they lived no farther away than a
bus ride.

"They're paid five pounds a night," said the manager in reply to
my query. "It's six thirty till nine then they lock up the turnstiles
and come up here with the takings," he continued.

"Have you stopped to wonder why middle aged blokes leave the
comfort of their firesides and travel, in some cases, fifty miles here
and back, for ten quid a week?" I enquired.

It seemed to take an age for the penny to drop, then he asked
me whether I thought there was someone amongst them who was
dishonest.

"Well, if you call pocketing the entrance fee of every other one
passing through his stile dishonest, the answer is yes indeed," I
observed.

He didn't ask me to take any further action in the matter, and
when I saw him again some weeks later he told me that he had
retired the turnstile staff and had installed fool proof machinery
to remedy the situation. I'm afraid that it would probably have
been outwitted within a short period of time and he would be back
to his shortfall, such is human nature, but I refrained from telling
him.

Actions, or omissions from the past, are wont to catch up with
us all, and in the case of policemen, more often than most.
Usually the original mistakes, like those of surgeons, stay buried,
and in the interest of everyone are best forgotten.

On one of those dark miserable wet evenings which always

seemed to be part of the make up of Manchester, my cape weighed down by the collection of water in its effort to keep the uniform underneath at least dry, but failing to protect my trousers from the thighs down being soaked, I trudged through the puddles abounding the pavements of my beat. Just after seven I passed the terraced house of a young woman who was well known as a club entertainer. She was standing at her front door, her pet dog underneath her arm and as I went by she greeted me.

"Hello Dennis," she called. "Wet enough for you?"

I waved to her and head down pushed on against the brisk breeze now pressing the rain against my front. At that stage a taxi drew up at her front door and the man I knew as her partner staggered from the vehicle, and in a series of short runs forward and back, clambered awkwardly through the doorway and into the house. His arrival had been greeted by a few strong words of disapproval on behalf of the lady, after which the door was slammed with unnecessary ferocity.

Some ten minutes later, at the end of the street, I could make out the flashing blue light on the police pillar, calling me to answer the telephone therein. The message was for me to attend the address of the popular singer I had but recently hailed, as an ambulance was on the way. On my arrival, I found the ambulance crew loading the man I had seen trying to negotiate his way in to the address.

"He's had it!" said one of the crew.

I examined the deceased and saw at once, from the congealed blood in his ears, that he had suffered a fracture of the skull. Inside the cosy well appointed little house, the grieving partner was partaking of a large gin, and between gulps, she outlined what had happened.

"You saw the state he was in Dennis. He went upstairs and the dog ran up after him. I went to call it back down and as it ran between his feet, he fell back down the stairs."

She refreshed her glass from the bottle in her other hand and continued. "He came flying down the stairs and banged his head on the edge of the open front door. When I saw the blood running from his ears I rang for the ambulance."

After completing a detailed statement and inspecting the stair carpet, etc., I completed the Coroner's report to the effect that the incident was the result of the man's drunken condition and his encounter with a small poodle.

I saw little of the woman after that apart from her occasional appearances at my favourite club. After promotion to sergeant and on to another division some twenty years passed. I was carrying out a period of duty as the Plain Clothes Sergeant, and in my capacity of regulating licensed premises I had occasion to visit a large pub where regular concerts took place. I noted that the licensee was in fact the entertainer who's unfortunate partner had so tragically passed away all those years before and as I entered the premises on an extremely busy night, I saw my old acquaintance. She occupied a kind of throne, surrounded by a crowd of admirers, some of whom I recognised from the world of show business.

As I approached she was taking a swig from a large silver goblet, which I later discovered, was kept charged with gin.

"Dennis!" she screeched, waving me over. "Come and sit down."

She instructed a waiter to attend to my every need, and I asked for a pint of bitter.

"Get him anything he wants; anything do you hear?" were her instructions.

I was somewhat embarrassed by her bawling and bowled over by the announcement she next made.

"You knew I'd pushed the drunken bastard down the stairs and you made out it was a bloody accident for me!"

The loudness of the music at that point seemed to have obliterated the proclamation from the hearing of those close by and I left the building promptly.

A few weeks later I heard that the flamboyant confessor, having suffered a heart attack, had passed on to that great musical hall in the sky.

Chapter Twelve

The old copper who, as his retirement drew near, was put out to grass as the Station Officer, stretched out in the chair of the tiny office.

"Yes, I've worked under some cute sergeants in my time," he said, "but the one I'm going to tell you about ought never to have been trusted out without his mother. A good many of the old sergeants had fads, but this one was cuter than all the lot put together."

The station constable eased his great bulk from the chair and ambled in to the kitchen.

"Fancy a cup o' tea?" he asked, to which I nodded and took a seat at the dining room table. "I was a green recruit when I first came to work on his section, and at that stage I didn't know what his hobby was. I was standing at my rendezvous point, right on time and I saw him walking towards me. 'All correct sergeant,' I said, to which he nodded."

I enquired about the sergeant's hobby, and he explained that it was borrowing money and failing to pay it back.

"He tapped the younger officers mostly, because they'd be a bit worried about asking for it back," he said. "There was no point making yourself unpleasant about it as he could be fifty times more unpleasant, as many a publican discovered, and provided he hadn't borrowed too much it could amount to be a sort of insurance.

"Sometimes, when walking round your beat, individuals would enquire as to where the sergeant was working and which shift he was on, to which a wise reply was to the effect that you had no idea."

I was called to the telephone and informed of an incident requiring my attendance so that it was a number of days later when I had the opportunity to listen to more of the sergeant's hobby.

"Now then, where was I up to sarge?" asked the old constable, as he swept the front step of the station. I reminded him that nobody disclosed where the sergeant might be, for fear of repercussions.

"That's right," he said, as he leaned heavily on the brush. "I think one of the best things he ever did was the way he got his front room and hall decorated for nowt, though that wasn't actually a matter of borrowing, more a confidence trick which he was also good at.

"Apparently his missus had been moaning for some time for him to buy some paint and wallpaper, and get down to smartening the home up. Around that time he made the acquaintance of a bloke who was in business as a painter and decorator. The man was an enthusiastic snooker player, and could be found on most evenings at the Boilermaker's Social Club just up the road here.

"One evening on the sergeant's day off, he turned up in there, and to the astonishment of the steward, bought himself a pint and another for the decorator, who was practising a few shots at the table. Well one thing led to another and the pair played a couple of frames which resulted in the sergeant losing miserably."

I had to wait until the constable had finished dealing with a member of the public who had called to report her dog missing, then he continued.

"I heard that the sergeant returned to the club the next day, where he again treated the decorator to a pint, waiting till the two glasses were filled, however, before whispering to the steward that he had inadvertently come out without his money. Promising to pay at a later date, he played another couple of frames, making doubly sure to lose both, after which he made arrangements for his new friend to do the decorating of his home. The painter told one of our lads months after carrying out the work, that he had finished up not only doing it for nowt, but purchasing all the materials as well."

One of the other beat men came into the station in order to partake of his supper, and the station officer informed him that he had been relating the tale of the free wall papering and painting job transacted by the old sergeant, and when the station officer left to answer the telephone the beat man picked up on the story.

"I called in to the Boiler Maker's and the decorator was there," said the officer. "He said that after he finished the job, which took him all of nine days, he handed the invoice to the old bugger when he saw him in the club. His esteemed customer bought him a pint and got himself a tomato juice, after which he bought him a fur-

121

ther four pints then he challenged him to a game of snooker. The match began and the painter, due to another pint and a large whisky from his generous friend, appeared to have lost his touch.

"He told me that the sergeant suggested an added interest and that if the decorator won the next frame he would pay him double the amount on the bill, but if his opponent lost he was to cancel his fee. The poor man, not realising that whilst he himself was very drunk and hardly in a condition to concentrate on his shots, agreed, the sergeant who was disgustingly sober won the match outright."

At the return of the station officer there began a general discussion on the matter. " He had obviously planned the whole thing from the outset," I said.

" That's right sergeant," said the station officer.

"Of course he never went near the Boilermaker's Club ever again and the steward never misses an opportunity to mention that he supplied the drinks for the deception, on a promise from the sergeant that he would pay for them the next time he came in."

Police officers such as that old rogue were few and far between, whilst the rest of us, though from time to time Satan himself was sent to try us, trod the road of integrity.

I had moved to a different section of the division and after a couple of weeks was still trying to familiarise myself with its topography. I had noticed an old woman, somewhat bedraggled and a little eccentric as she wandered about the district at all hours, always carrying a battered old shopping bag.

"She's part of the furniture sergeant," said the station officer, when I mentioned her to him.

Sometime around three in the morning I picked up the probationary constable who was on patrol in the Levenshulme area, and as we walked together the elderly woman shuffled towards us. She was carrying the well worn bag as usual and I informed the officer that she was a local person, who was a little eccentric and harmless, and that during his service it would be as well to recognise odd people as such.

I left the youngster to carry on with his beat and repaired to the small section station where I sat down whilst the station officer prepared a mug of tea for me. About ten minutes later, the probationer came in accompanied by the old woman we had discussed earlier.

"What are you doing with her?" I asked, openly annoyed at him for interfering with her after explaining her situation to him.

"It's 'cos of her shopping bag sergeant," the officer replied, and with that, he tipped the contents out on to the table. There were bundles of one pound and five pound notes, each roll secured by an elastic band. The station officer, a man getting on towards the end of his service, found it necessary to sit down immediately in order to cope with a sudden weakening of the knees, whilst I spilled the best part of half a mug of tea.

"I got talking to her, sergeant, and took a peep in to her bag. I thought it best to bring her in here and see what you thought I should do about it." said the probationer proudly. I told him that he must sit down and count the contents of the bag, enter the amount in his notebook and after returning it all to the bag, guard it with his life. I followed the station officer into the front office where I found him frantically puffing on a cigarette and wiping a stray tear from his eye.

"That old girl has been mooching about round here at all times of the day and night for six years that I know of, and probably a damn sight before that," moaned the constable. "I must have walked past her hundreds of times when she has been humping that bag of cash."

"You mean you're bitterly disappointed that you never had an opportunity to advise her I suppose." I suggested.

"Summat like that sarge," he replied.

A voice from the refreshment room had me back in there, where I found the old woman quietly singing and the probationer, his notebook held up for my inspection.

"It's four thousand and forty seven pounds sergeant. I've written it all down for you, and as you can see I put it all back in to her shopping bag."

I enquired whether or not he had managed to obtain her address from her, and he replied that he had.

"It's over Stockport Road just on the D Division."

The three of us, plus the bag of money, set off for the address she had given, to find that it was the home of her sister and husband. We got the couple out of bed, and in the cramped front room of the terraced property, I explained the purpose of the visit. The other woman showed no surprise that her older sister was in the habit of walking the district at night with a lot of money loosely conveyed in such an insecure fashion.

"We're always telling her about it," said the husband of the sister."

"But do you realise...have you any idea how much she's got in this tattered shopping bag?" I asked.

"Yes, " said both relatives in unison. "There's four thousand and forty seven pounds. When our dad died he left us the shop we all lived in and that was her share. I bought this place with some of mine and I've got the rest in the bank. Gerty here don't trust banks so she's preferred carrying it round with her for the past seven years," explained the sister.

In the end I persuaded Gerty to take the money to her sister's bank the next morning and her sister to make certain that she did so.

"There are people who I know would have taken all that cash from her, if only they could have guessed that it was in her shopping bag," I said.

"And probably spent it all on cigs and beer," said the probationary constable, with more understanding than I would normally have given a lad so young in the game and whom from that moment on I knew had the makings of a good policeman.

It was often quite easy to spot a probationary constable who was going to get on in the service, but sometimes when deciding that an individual appeared to have little chance of ever becoming a fully fledged police officer I was proved wrong, and in at least four such cases my assessment well and truly off the mark as the officers concerned went on to very high rank; never actually improving but nevertheless retiring with a much healthier pension than my own!

In the main, those who through hard work and devotion to their job achieved high rank were to be admired if, from time to time, somewhat reluctantly. One officer, who rose to chief superintendent and was extremely unpopular, retired to his former village in Scotland and within a few months died and was buried there.

An inspector who had been touring the Highlands whilst on holiday had stayed, quite by chance, at a pub in that very village.

"The wife and me were in the bar one evening when it came out that I was a Manchester policeman. The landlord told us that one of their local lads had been in the bobbies in Manchester, and when he mentioned his name I spilt the best part of half a pint down my jumper. It was MacNoone he was talking about."

I was surprised at what he was telling me, because the day after he retired he just seemed to disappear from the face of the earth.

124

"Not that anyone cared," I said.

"The next lunchtime, after a load of bitter, I went round to the Kirk, found his grave, and peed on it," said my friend, with an air of the utmost satisfaction.

I look back on my time as a Manchester policeman with a lot of great memories and would do it all over again, but not under the present day restrictions mind you.

As a serving officer informed me recently: "They'd sack you in your first week!"

If you have enjoyed reading this book, then you will certainly enjoy reading

On The Beat

True tales of a former Manchester policeman
By Dennis Wood

The first book written by former Manchester police officer Dennis Wood tells many fascinating and hilarious tales of his days pounding the beat in a city where policing had remained virtually unchanged for more than a century. Meet the quirky characters encountered by Dennis, (and that includes colleagues!) as he helped police the city between 1950 and 1975. A wonderful social history of an era now gone for ever.

£5.99.   ISBN: 1 874712 77 8   104pp

Also available

Just a Cop

True tales of a former
Philadelphia police officer
By John E. McLaughlin

This book tells, in hilarious fashion, the way the ordinary cop worked his beat, dealt with troublesome senior officers, and handled criminals – everything, in fact, from thieves to killers and rioters. Told in a simple, down to earth way, this book will delight anyone keen on police memoirs in a major American city.

£8.88 ISBN: 1 874712 71 9   196pp

The World of Crime

By Peter Riley & Mark Llewellin
Foreword by Edward Woodward

Tales of Victorian and Edwardian crimes always fascinate the public and this collection is no exception. It offers a wide range of true cases from the UK, the USA, Canada and France, including the infamous H.H. Holmes, Brides in the Bath and Lizzie Borden cases. With 95 illustrations, this large format book is a must for any true crime collection.

**144pp. £12.99 hardback   £9.99 paperback
ISBN: 1 874712 67 0 (hardback)
ISBN: 1 874712 74 3 (paperback)**

The Highways & Byways of Jack the Ripper

By Peter Riley

This modest book offers no new theory on the identity of Victorian England's most infamous killer. Instead the author outlines the case and lists the victims, but its main purpose is to offer readers the chance to visit, through contemporary photographs of the 1880s, the slums of Whitechapel and Spitalfields where the murders took place. The book also has a fine collection of photographs of the area as it looks today, with some comparison shots of the scenes then and now!

£4.99 40pp. ISBN: 1 874712 49 2
Book size: 21cms x 20cms

To order these titles send payment to
P & D Riley, 12 Bridgeway East, Runcorn, Cheshire WA7 6LD
or visit our website www.pdriley.co.uk